LOOKING

for a

SIGN

in the

WEST

a road poem by

PETER TUTTLE

BACK SHORE

First Edition

ISBN 0-9670981-2-2

Cover art and Back Shore *Wave* logo copyright 2003 by Edith Tuttle. Used by permission.

Book design by Ruth Maassen
Rockport, Massachusetts

Printed in the U.S.A.

Also by Peter Tuttle:
Pigeon Cove
Desire

Back Shore is a writers' collaborative. Peter Anastas, editor.

Back Shore
PO Box 211
Gloucester, Massachusetts 01931-0211

Telephone: 978-283-4582

Roads Taken

*For Edie
and for Betty
and Tut*

Blackened Rockfish

Headlights writing across
Still firs
(Or were they
Pines)
I don't know
Never been here
Before
Never been on a
Road like this
Before
Either
Endlessly
Seemingly endlessly
Tossing back and forth
Across the flanks of the
Black mountains
Feel like a
Small boat in a
Big storm
And
Truth is
She's one step
Away from
Well
Queasy
All that
Back and forth
She's never
I've never
We've never been on a
Mountain
Mountains
Like this before
Back where we
Come from
Came from
You didn't have
Mountains like this
Back there
You went up

You went down
End of story
Nothing like this

Kid at the gas station in
Willits says it's gonna take oh
Ninety minutes—two hours for
What looks as the crow flies or
Even as the crow might
Walk no more than
Say
Thirty miles
I assume the kid
They're all kids now
And we're their parents
I assume the kid's
Well
Doesn't look like he's on
Drugs
Seems like a nice enough
Kid
Polite
Forthcoming your
Basic all american white
Doing this for extra money or a
First car teenager up there
Back there in
Willits
Which we left at dusk
Thinking
Thirty miles
What's thirty miles
Surely not 90 minutes much less
Two hours *he* must be
Mistaken but no
Now that we're on this
Road we begin to
Understand in a way that
We did not understand
Before that we are not
Not in Minnesota nor
Even our before that and

(We thought) somewhat
Mountainous New
England

Any

More

Headlights writing on
Still firs or
Maybe they were
Pines
Never been
Never ever been
Anywhere like this
Before and
In truth
I must admit
It somewhat
A little bit
Somewhat *scared me*
The unknown
Unfamiliar
These mountains that go so
On and on
Up and down and
Over and around on
Tight hairpin curves where the
Signs say
And mean
5 MPH
And you think
How can they
I didn't know that they
Why would they
Build roads with curves so
Tight that you can only
Take them at
5 MPH
But there we were and you

Took them any faster and the
Tops of those firs rising from
Far below so that the
Upper branches brushed by the
Side of the road
In that black night
Those black
Mountains no lights for
Miles and miles and
Miles
There's no houses no cars
No *nothing* around here
Just forest and us on this
Now dark night
Not even *night* yet
Evening
We left Willits at seven
Figured Fort Bragg by
Eight but here we are
No road signs even to
Tell you how far
How where
Just this endlessly
Seems like
Never endingly
Hairpinning
Road curving
Tucking
Conforming to the
Infinite folds of the
Flanks of these mountains
Black with those tall
Not even shadowy but
Pure black trees
Just beyond the
White line lit
Edge of the road and
These
Reflective gizmos
Yeah
Kinda pop-up
Reflective gizmos down the

Center of the road
No one else
On the road so we
Take it all
Such as it is
Narrow road
Take it all for ourselves
This endless
Seems like
Endless
Tossing back and
Forth from one
Superelevated sharp
Almost impossibly
Sharp
(How do trucks get around
These) curve to another
Eyes almost
Mesmerized by the
Reflective gizmos and
You know
There's no doubt
You can see from those
Tops of the trees
What lies just beyond those
Headlights constantly writing
What
I didn't know
Some
Indecipherable
Prophecy on that
Wall of black
Trees
The firs
Or pines
I'm not sure
Maybe both
Imperturbable
Non reflective
Just black dark
But it's not
Entirely

Unknown
We know what lies
Right beyond the
Side of the road
There's the
Tops of those
Trees rising from that
Steep mountainside so
In other words
For a car and its
Occupants
What lies beyond
Just off the side of the
Road
For them
For us
What lies there is the

Abyss

She's driving
Just as well
Keep her eyes
Focussed on the
Center of the road
On those
Reflective gizmos as the
Car lurches and sways tossed by those
Superelevated curves she can
Keep her eye on the
Center like a
Twirling ballet dancer always
Watching that one point her
Head always snapping round
So she's driving while I
Wonder what it would
Be like trying to
Say
Change a tire with the car on a
Compound curve of grade and

Superelevation
(Means the side of the road is
Higher than the center
You know like an
Oval racetrack to
Help keep you from
Driving off the
Edge)
I keep thinking I've
Never changed a
Tire on this car before and
Imagining what it would be
Like to try to
Haul all that stuff out
Then on
No level surface
Jack the thing up and
Car would probably come
Crashing down on me
And
There I'd we'd be
The intrepid
Explorers
Latter day gold rush
Adventurers as
Ill-prepared as
Most of those
Gold rushers were and
I must confess
Somewhat motivated
(I was
She just
Believed in me)
By the same at once
Base and
Wonderful motives
The big risk
Big chance
Leave it all
Behind and
Go to *See the*
Elephant out

There
Out west
Where no one
Except one uncle
Has ventured
No one from *my* family has
Ventured before
Hell they don't
Probably can't even find
On the map where
Minneapolis is much less
Well
They know California
Which has had
Ever since
Much better press than
Minnesota
Where we now live
Sorta by default
We were looking for
Anonymous
Quiet
A sorta seclusion and
God knows we
Found very nice people but if you aren't
Sure where
Well—
Point is we had
Started west
Cut ourselves loose from
Three hundred fifty
Years of ties
Back east and
Launched ourselves
Set ourselves adrift
More like it
On the vast western
Continent and
Ended up working in
Minnesota but
Somehow
That love of the

Domestic
Well
That wasn't us
We'd cut ourselves loose and joined the
Westward drift and
Henceforth
Every chance we got
We had no choice
We were
Drawn
Impelled
West
Feeling as if we'd
Left one home
Back east and that
Somehow
Somewhere
The west
Could be
Should be
Had to be
Where else were we
Going to go
Wanting to make
Feeling that we had no choice
But to make
Believing that
Somewhere in that west
Mythic or
Otherwise
Somewhere
Out there
Out west was the
Place we should
Would want to
Would know
Recognize
Accept
Embrace as our new

Home

Then
Then
She says

The salt air
I can smell the
Salt air

And she opened the car window on her side and
Breathed deep and yes
Then even I
That seduction of fog and damp and salt and
Buoy's toll up there in the
Mountains
We must have crossed the last ridge and the
Trees out there
Still black now
Glistened in the
Writing headlights and I
Should have known
Though I didn't that we
Would always go back to
Salt water but what I
Thought at the time was
Oh great
Move 1400 miles to the
Middle of the continent only so
You can establish a sort of
Base camp there for
Further exploration
Still searching and the
Minute you get anywhere near
Salt water
She's

She's

Not sure I even
Told myself then
Wanted to admit or was
Able to acknowledge we'd only been

Gone from the east coast
Specifically
Rockport, Massachusetts
More specifically that
Part of Rockport known as
Pigeon Cove and
I thought
We thought at least
I thought *we* thought that we were
Destined for parts
Unknown the
High hinterland the
Great west where you
Lost yourself
Your old self
Pike's Peak or Bust and
Remade yourself a new
One
Was not so much that the
West coast
Those black trees
Those endlessly
Seemingly endlessly
Convoluted mountains seemed
Anything like
Quaint settled safe completely known
Where our ancestors had been for 350 years
New England but a
Coast that
Salt
Air
Her
Yearning
I didn't want to
Go back
More or less a
Failure back
There and a
Feeling of
Not belonging so
I did
We did

What all those other
Go West, Young
(Or not so young)
Men had done and
Turned our backs on
All we knew and
(As I might think of it much later)
Drifted on a high tide all the
Way up the Mississippi to the
Falls of St. Anthony
Head of navigation and caught on a
Snag so to speak
Beached the boat and
Bought an utterly totally completely
Anonymous home in
Plymouth, Minnesota a
No there, there kinda
Town if there ever—
Did I say *Town*
Not hardly
Creation of real estate developers and
Ringed by access roads and all new houses and
For us a
Perfect place to
Hide out
Nobody knew us
Many many many miles from the
Old homes and families and
From there
From that base camp
(You wouldn't call it a
Home)
We could
We did
Every chance we got
Keep on
Searching

The salt air
The black trees

Glistening now as
Trees should with that
Fog *off the ocean*
And no longer now even so
Black that
Disturbing unfamiliar
Black I had never
Seen trees that
Black before because always
Always they'd have this
Glistening of moisture
Fog moist just air off the
Ocean and the mist fog
Moisture also present
Comforting soft gentle
Visible among the branches so that
Even on the darkest night when the
Headlights wrote them you saw not
Pure black but hints of green and
Even in dead of night
Faint gray
That black
That abyss of the
Edge of the road
Unfamiliar that
In some way
Not physically but
Emotionally had
Scared me

Road levels now
Mailboxes
Civilization again
We of the sissy east and
Settled midwest aren't accustomed to
Miles and miles of
Nothing but black trees and
5 MPH curves with
Precipitous drops off the
Edges of the mountains

All new to us
We'd scrawled across half the
Continent on the interstates the
Beautiful interstates
Four lanes wide and
You can see forever into the
Future
Relatively speaking
Miles ahead
Most places and it had been
Fun
It had been easy
We *liked* the interstates
So different from back east
(Should we capitalize *Back East*)
Sort of an all-encompassing term for that
Place where we no longer were
No longer felt we belonged
No longer felt we were part of
Uprooted now like those
Mormons with their
Pushcarts and those
Fortyniners travelling
Any way they could even by
Stagecoach as had
Some years later
Overland stage
Mark Twain in *Roughing It*
(A lot less rough than it had been
If you could even travel by stage) and his
Complaint about the Platte River
Everyone's complaint *A*
Mile wide and six inches deep
He rode
We drove for
Miles and miles and miles beside the
River Platte
Platte River Valley
All through Nebraska the land
Rising imperceptibly
Becoming drier imperceptibly
But you don't notice because of the

River
The river valley
If you can call what seems like
Dead flat a valley
The river
Bearing moisture
Deceives you
Keeps the land green long after
The rest
Beyond has become more
Arid and then
Suddenly
Around Julesburg, Colorado
Not far from the Nebraska/Colorado line
(And it's amazing how despite the
Apparent arbitrariness of those
Rectangular states the
State lines really do denote some
Geographic change)
Suddenly at Julesburg
For us around 1 am
Been driving all day and
Half the night from
Minneapolis
Completely unable to stop
Pure road scrawl
Once we started we could no more
Stop than—
Kept going after supper in Grand Island
Nebraska then on into the
Gathering western dark and
On and on
Me driving now
She asleep with the
Silver of moon
Dusting her shoulder and the
Sage
Perfume of sage that
Clear clean dry high plains almost
Desert smell
Pure western
The smell of the west

Suddenly
In the dark
Around Julesburg
No lights anywhere the
Farms have turned to
Ranches and spread themselves
Far apart on the
High range there and
Suddenly that
Sage in the
Air and you knew
I knew that now we were in the
West

Denver, friends then west through
Utah
Some stretches of no civilization
(Apart from the 4 lane) in
Utah
Some 200 miles of it
San Rafael Swell
But still the
Comforting big road the
Interstate upon which there were
Almost always
Other cars
Other people
Nothing like these hours of
Night and black trees over the
Coast Range from Willits and now
Down
Mailboxes appearing at the sides of the road
Grades easier
No more lurching curves
Salt air in the trees and the
Signs
US 1
Left (south) toward Mendocino and
Right (north) toward Noyo
Fort Bragg where
We'd been told by friends who

Emphatically *had not driven across*
Half the continent just the usual
East coast sissies who
Flew out to Frisco and piddled around in a
Rented car not
Carrying half their goods and chattel
An entire miniature household in the
Back of their car as we were
Semi true immigrants given that we
Still had that base camp
So to speak in Minn
But these friends as I
Started to say had told us about the
Wonderful restaurant the
Likes of which you would never
(Well, they would never) expect in a
Small sawmilling and somewhat tourist town
Miles and miles north on the
Lost foggy north coast of
California where one
Evening they had just
Stumbled in looking for
Someplace to eat and where they had
On a whim ordered the
House special
Blackened Rockfish and it had
Been the *best*
One of the best if not the
Best meals in a restaurant that
They had ever eaten
Which was why to get
Back roughly to where we
Started we had continued driving
On through the dark
Just thirty more miles
From Willits on
(As we soon realized) the
Other side of the Coast Range to
Fort Bragg because it was
Then about 7 pm and we figured
Heck
Good restaurants usually stay

Open even at least until 8
And heck
We'll be there in no time and
We can after this
Long road scrawl across
Half the continent
Reward ourselves by
Sitting down in a
Good restaurant
(We had seen our share
En route of
McDonalds) and
Just as
David and Janis Newcomb our
Friends from Reading, Massachusetts had
Told us to do
We would
Sit ourselves down at this
So they said
Wonderful restaurant and
Ask for
Hope for
The House Special:
Blackened
Rockfish

Main Street
Fort Bragg
Lumber town
Fishing nearby and that
Seduction of salt air
Perspiring in the
Open car windows
The damp
The gentle mist you
Don't get anywhere else
Soft air in what was here a
Soft dark but not
Black night with the
Buildings
Most of them
Closed up tight for the
Weekday evening
No traffic
Streetlights shiny in the
Street and the
Ford dealership
Art deco as I
Recall once home to Model As
Now a new Thunderbird and we
Parked nearby for
Across the street
Pretty much right across the
Small main street
From our destination
The Restaurant
Site of *Blackened Rockfish* that
Dave and Janis Newcomb had
Praised so highly and
Yes
They were still open
This quiet weekday evening
Still open
A few diners/ couples inside
Place not fancy but cozy
Natural wood high ceilings
Fishing stuff (as I recall) on the
Walls and the picture of a man in his

Middle years gazing directly at the
Camera
No compromise there
The owner
I guessed
And the pleasant sounds of
Competent cooking coming from the
Kitchen at the back not so
Much loud as audible only because
The town
The other diners
So quiet
Low lighting
Banquettes
Where we sat down
Guided by the (young) hostess and
Yes they were still open
If barely
Almost 9
We'd just made it and there
On the blackboard
Special of the Day

Blackened Rockfish

A wine

The waitress asks and
After that long difficult drive
Across the Coast Range
Not to mention that fairly long if not
Difficult drive across
Half the continent in
Not too many days
Long days
The continent unfolding
Beneath us a
Geography lesson beneath our
Tires
Yes

We were ready for a
Glass of wine or
Maybe two and so

Frog's Leap
Sounds neat

She says and I
Agree

But it's
Not cheap

We're worth it

And besides it's
Almost our
Anniversary

Sixteen if you
Can believe it I can now but it
Seemed not so much a *long* time as a
Short wonderful time and it was
Hard to believe that many—

So
Frog's Leap

Which arrives in a bottle with an
Elongated leaping frog on the
Label and Mark Twain would have been
Proud this
California wine after his
California story
That was
Of course the
Whole idea behind
California
Behind going to
California to make this

Leap

They *leapt* over half the
Continent to get there paying no
Attention whatever to all of that
Geography in between which was
Strictly an impediment and the
Idea was
Of course
Once you made it to
California you then
Leapt into
Riches and
Lived happily
Thereafter
Living your dream

For that was the
Idea about California you
Moved there and
Proceeded to
Live your dream and as we
Would soon discover in
Virtually any conversation with
Any Californian about their
Lives the whole idea
The spirit of the place
The accepted and expected
Curriculum vitae almost
No matter what was not
Going back to the way things used to be or
Trying to fit into some preordained
Establishment or hierarchy but to
Live
Yours truly
Individual
Nobody else's
Dream

That was what you did there and
I dunno
Did we really

Know what our dream was
Did we know *where* our
Dream was

No
That's what we were on the
Road to find out but we did know
That evening as
First the salad and then the
Main course the
Blackened Rockfish
Arrived that the present
Could not have been
More
Wonderful
And we
She and I
Gave thanks for those
Sixteen years
Together and
For dark night and the
Long ride over the mountains and for the
Perspiration of fog and the
Salt air
All that combined into a
That evening
That evening
Drinking the wine of the
Frog's Leap and eating

Blackened

Rockfish

Another Round

Stagecoach lanterns
Writing in the
Wild eyes of a
Six horse team
Plunging down the
Geiger Grade some
Autumn night like
This one the desert air so
Clear you could
Stand on an A Street cottage
Porch on the high flank of
Sun Mountain and see the
Lights writing from
Austin on the side of
Lander Hill 175
Miles away or perhaps
See the ghost of
John Millian hanged for
Murder of the prostitute the
Well liked humane middleaged
Prostitute named Julia Bulette a
Crib girl or
Perhaps we should say
Crib woman who made her
Living in a one room shack in a
Row of one or two room shacks on
Notorious D Street in a town where
Most of the streets were in
Some way
Notorious for this was
Virginia City
So named for one of the
Luckless prospectors who originally
Found the gold and true to the
Hapless prospector tradition
Lost it to smarter miners and
Investors who shortly
Thereafter came along to
Mine the Comstock Lode a
Vein of silver ore so

Rich that it singlehandedly
Funded much of the
Union War effort in the
Far off east coast while
Mark Twain younger brother of Abe Lincoln-appointed
Orion Clemens got a gummint job
Young Mark drifted from
Gold camp to gold camp
Prospecting fruitlessly and
Sending in the occasional
Piece to the *Territorial Enterprise*
Biggest newspaper west of the Mississippi
For the Comstock Lode had built a city
Virginia City on the
Eastern flank of a desert mountain in
Western Nevada where they
Brought water in by a flume from the Sierra Nevada some
20 miles away and
Lumber from the Sierra Nevada by flume and
Railroad the
Virginia and Truckee railroad
Richest short line in North America in
Its time and now all but a small short section
Rebuilt for the tourists long gone but
Virginia
Virginia City was
Still there in all her
Decrepit glory the ancient wood and brick
Buildings with their tall
Angular Victorian facades
Perched unsteadily on the
Flanks of the unsteady
(Thanks to the miles of tunnels
Dug beneath it) mountainside and
Where some twenty thousand or more
Temporary citizens had lived amid
What amounted to an urban
Civilization in the middle of the
Desert a
Fabulous city like something out of the
Old Testament before God's wrath or the
Hittites' or Hebrews' wrath

Sodom and or Gomorrah before the
Destruction
That was Virginia
Where the four story International Hotel had the
First elevator west of the Mississippi and
Anything you could want that could be
Bought and transported over the
Virginia and Truckee Railroad
Anything you could want in the way of
Movable luxury or a
Woman's flesh
Any woman's flesh
That was all available
At a price
Of course but the
Miners had the money
Paid $4 per day
The kings of skilled labor in
Those days and the
Men living like Croesus
Comparatively speaking
They had the money though one of the
Things that strikes you in a
Place like that was how little
Really of the
Money stayed there
The so-called *Mansions* still there
Nothing more than large Victorian houses
Big compared to miner's shacks but nothing more than
Pieds a terre for the
Rich owners who built their
Real mansions on
Nob Hill in San Francisco and sent
Daughters to Europe to marry
Royalty while the lode the
Fabulous Comstock Lode gradually
Played itself out until the
Ore wasn't rich enough to
Cover the cost of digging it out in the
Ever deeper mines and the water
Mineral laden that
Bubbled up from deep within the

Earth gradually filled those
Miles and miles of timber-lined tunnels in the
Unstable earth once the
Pumps shut down so that
Now when you toured the mine
As you walked in the horizontal drift into the
Complete darkness within the
Mountain a steady trickle of
Water ran out a hose from a pump and
Even that shaft too would be
Filled and
Once you were in there
Some couple hundred feet the
Guide
First turns off the electric lights and
Then
Blows out the candle
And it's darker than you have
Ever seen dark before there is
No light and you
Cannot see your hand in front of your
Face and I reached for
Her hand and she
Reached for mine and
Held tight
While the guide said
And how much am I
Offered to light the
Candle?

Footsteps resounding on wooden sidewalks under
Wooden awnings hanging from
Elaborate brick facades of the
Ghost town after it was rebuilt from one of the
Innumerable fires that swept through those
Gold and silver camps all built of
Lumber buildings jammed one next to
Another in that era of no water mains and
Horsedrawn fire equipment back when

Fire companies were young men's social clubs
Each with their distinctive uniforms and
Insignia and the firehouse where the
Steam powered horsedrawn
Fire pumps resided shiny nickel and brass and copper
Fittings the latest and most modern
Technology but
Nothing that would put out a fire in a
City of wooden shacks and shops where
Every last building was heated by a wood or
Coal burning stove
Our footsteps resounding in the
Dark we had the town pretty much to ourselves that
October night what with the day tourists
Virginia was strictly a day tourist town
The busloads arriving from Carson from Reno
See the authentic wild west
Well it *was* the authentic wild west
Moreso than we even knew and the
Office of the *Territorial Enterprise*
Where Mark Twain worked
(Actually he worked in the
Wooden building that had preceded this brick one that
Burned down)
But the town that 1870s
Town had not changed much since then for it had
Steadily lost
Population as the mining declined until in that wellbuilt
Brick town center that had once served some
20,000 now only some 6-700
Remained
Small modern school building on the
Edge of town and the saloons
One after another lining the street
All had slot machines by the bar the
Bucket of Blood and all the
Rest this dark clear October night
Each saloon had
You could see it
Its small local clientele
Probably just as happy to
Have the tourists gone and the

Town back to themselves and we
Walked up and down the
Main street
C Street
Looking for someplace to
Sit ourselves down and nurse a slow beer
Or two
We didn't have to drive
Having set ourselves up to camp on the
Tailings dump turned
Campground and
RV Park as it
Proudly proclaimed itself on the
North side of town and
There we were the
Town pretty much to ourselves
Us and the locals and
Finally we saw a saloon that
Looked smaller and cozier
Just a few folks sitting at a bar and one
Heavy biker guy at the back and the
Barmaid
Young and pretty in a
Sort of western wear cowgirl's
Tailored shirtwaist dress with an
Open
Very open neck that
Left you in no doubt about the
Beauty of her breasts as she
Leaned over in
Front of us for
Something or perhaps for
Nothing at all and
Listed the beers
One of which was
Rattlesnake
From somewhere in Texas which
Sounded appropriately western to us and

Sure
Two Rattlesnakes

And I
We tried to engage the guy next to me in
Young man
Fit and tanned plaid shirt
In some kind of
Desultory conversation but
That was the odd thing about that
Bar
No one seemed to be engaging in
Much conversation it was as if
They were all
Waiting
But waiting for what we didn't know and
Barmaid and another young and
Seemingly unattached young woman
Engaged themselves in
Putting up Halloween decorations
Halloween is a big adult holiday out
West where the more religious and family holidays have
Never taken much hold
Particularly in towns like
Virginia City, Nevada
Where I was thrilled just because the
Place was so little changed from its
Days of glory
More decrepit of course but
Otherwise so little changed and
We sat there in that
Not unfriendly silence
Near silence
No one seemed to be
Paying much attention to the
Television and the
Young man to my right told me how
Some guy's old pickup truck
Parked on one of those
Precipitous streets had
Let go its emergency brake and
Rolled into the side of his
Brand new Toyota
Pickup truck
Precisely why I'd left our car

Back at the RV Park and
Anyway the walk did us good and
Then the young man and the barmaid began
Playing with a kitten that bounded into the next room and
Then up the stairs and the
Barmaid ran up the stairs
The young man following and then
Sometime later
Maybe 15 or 20 minutes
The barmaid returned downstairs
Handed a handful of
Bills to the bearded biker gent in the
Back of the bar and then she
Returned to the bar while
First adjusting her bra straps and then her
Garters and then
As she leans forward
Asks us

Another round?

Moonlight or
Maybe it was
Starlight gleaming in the
White crosses of the
Graveyard on
Boot Hill just across the
Canyon from us
From where we were camped on the
Edge of the flattened top of an
Immense tailings pile from a
Century of mining
Tailings pile now turned into this
RV Park with its
Reasonably authentic
Board and batten buildings the
Washhouse the office
Place virtually empty that night though
Off season
Way off season

Just us sleeping in the
Back of our station wagon
New station wagon
New Taurus station wagon
New Ford
Made us feel
Prosperous then which we were
Relatively if you
Can buy a new car
But then again
There we were
Sleeping in the
Back of the thing
Throw all the stuff
All our stuff
Clothes and other
Camping gear into the
Front seats for the
Night while we stretch
After a fashion
Out in the back
(Lucky she's petite)
Because we've got just
Six feet from the back of the
Front seats to the
Tailgate to
Stretch
After a fashion
Out in and
We lay there in our
Little used but not new
Down sleeping bags
Cozy in their warmth
Our warmth
She lying naked
Beside me
Tucked into the
Warm cocoon of that
Down while outside the
Washoe Zephyr as they
Call the local wind
Rocked the car

Literally and
Sent the
Dust flying
Rocked us as if we were at
Sea in a small boat and
Yet a not unpleasant feeling
What with the warmth of the down and
Warmth of her slim body and
Soft skin and beautiful
Curves beside me and
Though we were no longer
Young we were a heckuva
Lot younger then than we
Are now and
We still felt young
Poised just on the far edge of
Youth as we were poised at the
Edge of that tailings pile somewhere
Halfway between the beauty of
Youth
That young woman's youth
For instance
Though she beside me
Still looked
Young still had her
Twentyfive year old body but
We weren't young we
Were almost 40
Halfway
More or less
Halfway
If you're lucky
Leaving behind
Which we understood in a
Theoretical way
But did not feel
Did not yet feel
Still *felt* 26
And she still
Looked 26 and
Still felt 26
Her arms her hands her face her breasts

Her feet her legs her thighs
Her flesh
All around me as we
Rocked that car ourselves
Poised as it was on the edge of the
Tailings pile while
Below us and
Beyond there
Wrote the white
Crosses of
Boot Hill once including
Julia Bulette's
With its own little
Fence around it
Writing in the moonlight
But we
Paid them no mind
Almost no mind
Did not imagine
Not yet
Ourselves anyplace like
There as we
Rocked the car
Rocked the car again and
With the covers flung off
We lay there
For awhile
A little while and
Then she asks

Another

Round.

Right There

White owl standing on the
Broken white line
Running down the center of
US 50
Two lanes running
East/west across the
Center of the state from
Fallon to Ely with an
Assortment of
Mountain ranges but
Very few
Very few
Towns in between
Which was the reason
You saw
Sorta saw what with their
Reflective letters and
Some of the background
Dark all
Sandblasted through the
Years since they
Put them up
The big signs on the
Side of the road
Proclaiming
Quoting a *Life*
Magazine article to the
Same effect:

Loneliest Road in America

Then again
How could it be
What with the sign there
The *loneliest* road
You had the sign for company
Right there
Albeit a little
Sandblasted and in fact
Barely legible

But there
Nevertheless and I
Already knew in a
General way what to
Expect from US 50 for I had
Read all about it in one of
My favorite road books and
One of the best all time
(In my humble opinion) road books
Blue Highways by
William Least Heat Moon his
Native American name
How one spring after he'd
Lost his job and wife had
Run off or
Started to run off
Or things had just
Fallen apart between them he
Put his household into his
Ford Econoline van with a
Makeshift homemade
Bed arrangement in the back and
Spent six weeks on the road and then
Six years writing about it
Wonderful book
What was left of the country
Before the interstates *completely*
Changed the map and the
Small towns
Many of them had
Not yet dried up and
Died and
No I
Did not want to
Leave my wife behind to
Write an odyssey a
Search for the
Self of that kind I
Could not imagine
Did not anyway
Want to imagine going
Anywhere without my

Wife
We may have been
Looking for something but one
Thing we sure as heck were
Not looking for was
Each other
However
This night
This dark night
Sometime around
Oh
I dunno
Maybe 8 PM
There we were
Scrawling ourselves across the
Nevada desert with the
Prophecy of
Loneliest Road in America already
Unfulfilled
Too late
Rendered untrue by the
Fact of that sign being there and
Yet
Somehow
Maybe because I had
Simply thought about the place the
Chapter in Least Heat Moon's book
Describing his visit to
Frenchman, Nevada
Pop. 3 in the
Middle of the US Navy
Bombing range
Out there in the middle of the
Desert
His breakfast of milk shake from a
Mint green Hamilton Beach triple
Mixer and the account of their
Lives given by the family of 3
Living 50 miles by one road from the
Next town
For that reason and
That reason alone I

Wanted to keep going
Into the dark on this
Once loneliest road in America
Despite the signs
Bright yellow and black
Showing a rather frisky looking
Cow with the words
Open Range
Which
Indicates
(For all you who don't live or
Travel out west
Anywhere
Anytime)
That
No matter how fast you
Might be going
It is
Likely or at least possible
You will encounter
Cattle
Wandering across the unfenced road and in the
Minds of the law and
Certainly in the minds of the
Cattle and without question in the
Laws of physics
($F=MV$) the
Cattle
Not you the
Motorist have
Right of way
Even at the legal 55
MPH say which in
Broad daylight is
No problem and as we
Would learn on
Subsequent journeys you
Just say *What the hell* and
Do 80
Because otherwise you'd
Spend all day crossing desert with
No traffic and

Fifty miles between towns but at
Night
Any night but
Especially this
Dark
Autumn night
We were utterly
Damn fools to be doing
55 MPH or in fact
Any MPH
Hell I'd seen the
Pickups parked behind the
Garage in Fallon with their
Front ends stove in as if they'd
Rammed boulders when in
Fact what they'd rammed was a
Half ton or more of
(Formerly)
Ambulatory beefsteak
They like to
Stand on the road
These cool nights
Soak up the
Heat from the day from the
Macadam was the
Way the lady at the
Fallon gas station
Put it to me from
Behind the counter where she
Sold T shirts lettered
I Survived US 50
Which we hadn't yet so I
Didn't want to tempt fate by
Buying one and now as we
Saw that almost
Perfectly white
Bright white
Two foot or more high
Owl standing in the exact
Center of the road on the
Centerline of that otherwise
Inscrutable

Unreadable
Black pavement I began to think that my
Obsession with reaching and staying overnight at
Frenchman, Nevada that night was
Perhaps not the smartest thing in the
World to do but
By now
There we were
Halfway from Fallon to
Frenchman so we
Kept on driving knowing
Perfectly well
Understanding now
Perfectly well that if there was a
Large dark object in the
Shape of a non-reflective
Steer on the road and we
Hit it at 55-60 MPH in our
Little plastic and thin steel
Taurus that as the
Lady at the Fallon
Service station had
Told me it would be like
Ramming a
Brick
Wall

And then
And then as the
Road rose at first
Imperceptibly
And then
Then we began to
See them those
First large fluffy
Snowflakes appearing like

Messengers in front of the
Headlights and swooping by the
Windshield and at first I
Didn't think
Too much about it for
How far can we be from
Frenchman
Another couple miles
We'd been
Watching the odometer and yes
Then
There
Just about where we
Thought we ought to
See Frenchman
Nevada
Population 3
It was there
Off in the dark
Barely visible off the
Side of the road
You could make out the
Sand drifted flat areas where
Frenchman
Service station motel and
Café had all once been and
Yes
There
Standing like three
Sentinels there rose
What looked like
Three metal pipes
Standing upright in a
Small narrow island of
Concrete the old
Pump island
Most likely and

You think that was it?
I asked her not wanting to
Believe that brief glimpse that
Like one of those

Snowflakes or the
Big white owl had
Sped past my eyes in the
Opposite of my direction of
Travel and she replied
That's where it was
Supposed to be

And as we continued on
Down the road now faced with
Another mere 50 miles of
Open Range *not to*
Mention ever-thickening
Flakes these little but
Numerous messengers from that
Dark telling us
For one thing that

Frenchman wasn't

Frenchman

Anymore

Snow falling more
Rapidly now those
Large white fluffy
Messengers now
Covering the road and
Beginning to stick so that
Seeing the formerly
Bright white
Centerline began to
Become impossible and there was the
Additional consideration of
Traction

Now about an
Hour or two later as we were
Yes we were
Most definitely climbing and soon
Yes we were
There there it was
Austin, Nevada
Sprawled on the
Side of a mountain or anyway
Large hill some several
Thousand feet higher or
Anyway
Enough higher so that the road began
Climbing quite
Steeply past the old old
Stone and wood
Buildings that lined Austin's
Main Street
US 50 as it
Rose through town which was
Built in a
Gulch on a slant
Quite some slant known as
Pony Canyon for the
Pony Express route that
Once
Ran through here and
Now as we
Climbed I could

Barely see in fact
Couldn't really see beyond the
Hood of the car as those
Soft silent
Messengers came down
Thicker and thicker
Covering *everything in white so that I*
Had no idea where was the
Center of the road and
Where was the side
Town seemed
Closed up tight
No lights
Midnight or a
Little past it by now you
Don't get very far very fast
Travelling at 20 mph as
We had done for now some
Several hours just trying to
Reach Austin and now that we were
Here
Yikes
I couldn't see where to go
Where to turn off and I was
Afraid to stop for fear we'd
Slip and never get moving again be
Just stuck there in the
Middle of the road all night until
Someone rammed us and
Finally she
Leaned out her side of the car
Leaned out the open window into the
Storm and watched for a place
Any place to
Turn off I was
Driving blind by now and
She said as we
Crept upward
OK
Now
Coming up
Just make a sharp

Right turn when I say
Now

Which I did
Turning onto
Flat snowy ground and
Stopping
Gravel crunching under the tires
Under the snow and in the
Light reflected from our
Headlights
We couldn't see much but we
Could see a sign in
Not too bad repair
Reading
Joe Ramos' Trailer Court
This is it
We can't go
Further tonight and
She agreed so we
Pulled off to one side between some
Large semi-permanent none too new
House trailers and
Spread out our
Sleeping bags and
Turned in for
What was
Left of the
Night

Big American V-8 saying
Something underneath its
Breath woke me sometime
Later that night and I
Worried it might be
Law or someone who might
Call the law
People can get

Particular when you
Park on their land
Uninvited as of course we were
But then again
Out west
There's an understanding that the
Weather and land are
Dangerous and if you
Take shelter you're tolerated
Because whoever owns the place
Just might find himself or herself or
Themselves in the same
Fix sometime themselves so I
Wasn't as worried as much as I
Should have been but
Nevertheless could imagine some
Man of the law leaning down into the
Car
There we were
Naked under the sleeping bags
(We are too old for
Sleeping in the discomfort of our
Clothes) and having to
Explain
The storm
Couldn't see
Losing traction
Seemed easier to me to
Just dress and get up and
Wade through the now
It looked like
Maybe six inches of
Snow over to that trailer
Across the trailer park
Where a light now glowed and
Adjacent to which I
Assumed the V-8
Grumbled at having to
Arise so early in the
Cold and dark I know I
Would
So I did

Pulled on the jeans
Jacket over no shirt and
Waded through the snow in my
Inadequate shoes to
Explain myself to whomever at that
Very late or very early
Hour might be upset to
See us in their trailer park
So yeah
Through the snow
Into my shoes
Onto their makeshift porch and
There inside a middleaged
Guy in his underwear and shirt
Pulling on his pants completely
Oblivious to the possibility that
Then
In the dark in the
Middle of the night
Anyone *else* might be up or
What the hell
You're up that late
Who cares?
So I stepped back a
Moment until he'd finished
Dressing and then
Knocked lightly in
What I hoped was an
Unstartling manner and
Stood in the spill light from the door window and
Yes
He looked surprised but not
Angry or armed and
I explained
The storm
Couldn't see
Car sliding
And no he wasn't
Joe Ramos but he said
Joe Ramos doesn't
Want you to get in an
Accident you're all

Right don't worry about it
Stay

Right

There.

By Night

Wasn't the rain that bothered me
So much though the
Wipers couldn't keep up it was the
Hail coming down in
Fingernail size pieces any
Bigger and you could
Start to notice
Messages in your
Car and too much
Bigger and you could
Notice hieroglyphics in your
Windshield
Which made me nervous
Not used to
Weather like that
No one mentioned
Weather like that
Cold
Yes
Bugs
No
Hail
No
Tornadoes
No
This was all new and
Unwelcome to us
Not part of the
Adventure that we had been
Counting on
For it was an *adventure*
This living someplace
Different
So different from
Anything that we'd
Known before
Driving at night
Dumb to begin with
There's always deer on the
Road but the rain

Sheets of it washing down my
Windshield and the
Hail
Bouncing cheerfully off the hood like
Some kind of science experiment the
Wipers breaking up the bounces into
Discrete moments like a high school
Science lab stroboscope
Except that
No
I hadn't
We hadn't
Planned on being inside the
Experiment in this
Increasingly small glass plastic and metal
Not so sheltering cocoon and
Whyinhell
Anyway did we keep on going to
Glendive, Montana
When we could've stayed any number of
Places *before* it got dark
Dickinson, North Dakota for instance
Dickinson was a nice town with a
Nice friendly chicken place on the
Edge of town where those
Infinitely quiet infinitely reserved
North Dakotans came into town for
Saturday night and well
They may have raised hell *someplace*
But it sure as hell wasn't at
Jack's Restaurant where even the
Little kids were
Quiet
Patiently playing with
Bits of dough that the waitresses
Gave them
Making play dough effigies
While they
Waited with the grownups to be
Fed the iceberg lettuce
(Forgettable)
The rolls

Freshly baked and hot and then the
Chicken which was
No doubt
Very fattening but
Quite delicious
Eating it there with the
Late afternoon sun streaming in
Past the grain elevators and railroad
Tracks and into the western facing
Windows of Jack's
We could and
Shoulda
Stopped there but *no*
Another hour's light through the
Badlands and in the dark where we
Also coulda stopped
Medora, North Dakota former
Haunt of Teddy Roosevelt and on and
On in the dark toward those high dark clouds
Gathering in the west thinking we'd
Get as far as Glendive, Montana
Because it was the next place on the
Map
A lot of places you keep driving to
Out west simply because they're the
Next place on the map
Hard to imagine back east where there's
One town and then another with no
Nothing
In between but out west it's
Just the opposite there's a
Whole lot of *nothing*
Then a town
Maybe and then a
Lot more
Nothing in
Between
So the rhythm of travel is
Quite different
You drive and drive and drive and drive
Undisturbed by
Traffic

What *traffic?*
Undisturbed undiverted unencumbered by
Towns or houses or even, often, any
Ranches even except
Maybe for the fencing
Which *does not* keep the
Deer off the
Interstate and you
Drive and drive and drive
Another kind of existence
Really
You at once yearn for a town
Any town
That's what you're used to
Security
Help if needed and
Yet at the same time you
Realize when you
Finally arrive at one of these
Towns that you've truly been
Someplace else
Out there a
Someplace else you
Never really get to
Back east
Try to tell
Easterners about it and
Some of them
Many of them
Won't
Can't
Get it
You have
For a little while
Become one with
Not the towns
But the
Continent

Rain still coming down and
Hail
Hail pounding a message on the
Roof of our second story
Motel room somewhere on the
Outskirts of
Glendive, Montana
Sometime after midnight and
We're lying there wondering if the
Car's gonna be all right
How fast can you get a
1988 Ford Taurus windshield
Replaced in Glendive, Montana I
Wondered and no matter
What insurance pays you to
Fill all those messages with
Bondo a hail damaged
Vehicle is never gonna be the
Well we couldn't worry about it
Or shouldn't we were
Safe and dry in this little
Old fashioned not too many unit
Motel the kind with the outside shelf like
Balconies for access to your room
No hallways and this being
Montana the kind with
Electrical outlets in front of
Every parking space nosing
Up to the motel because
No doubt in this eastern Montana
High prairie country you got the
Same 20 or 30 or 40 below zero
Cold that graced Minnesota for
It seemed
Half the year
Well
No chance of that but this being
Montana
Eastern Montana
There we were worrying about
Balls of ice smashing up our
Car in the middle of

July

Still raining hard the next morning
Lightning thunder
Loud thunder as we
Scampered from car to
Arches
May not sound romantic to you but
Believe me
Arches can look
Pretty good in the
Middle of nowhere or
Almost nowhere and the
Fact is
Simple truth is
How much time you wanna
Spend looking for someplace different when
If there's an *Arches* there it
Usually means
That's where the townspeople
Now go also so you're
Not
Not usually
Gonna find that homey little friendly little
Gossip and chitchat laden little
Café that you used to find in every small town
Pre Arches
Cause the locals been eating there forever and
They were ready for a change and
So they make the new *Arches* usually
Out there by the exit and entrance ramps on the
Edge of town their
New local hangout and
Sit around happily drinking a
Single cup of coffee there or maybe there's a

Refill deal so if you're in one of
These small towns and you wanna
Hang around however
Briefly with the locals and
Soak up some of the
Atmosphere as best you can
You say to hell with it and
Drive to the local
Arches and
Run in through the raindrops
Building *literally* shaken by thunder
Right overhead as you
Step in the door dripping wet and
What was that says one of the
Locals who turns out to be a
Schoolbus driver but this is
Sunday so he's off and he and his
Buddies all men in
Late middle age
Old enough to know that
Unless they hit the
Lottery
This is it
So they might as well enjoy *it*
Even or especially on a
Rainy Sunday summer
Morning after a
Night of hail and downpour
Irrigation ditches filling
Even where they shouldn't
Maybe lightning hit a breaker
In the outskirts of town
Near the exit ramps in
Glendive, Montana

And you wonder
So what is it
Just a

Lottery

Or a

Pillar of

Cloud by

Day

And a

Scrawl of

Fire

By

Night.

What I Do

The wind wrote
Messages across those
Rolling hills of grain
Cat's paws across
Oceans and oceans of
Wheat
Far as we could see in
Every direction that
Bright cloudless blue sky
Noon in downtown
Sprague, Washington
Pop. Not Too Many
Just the block or two of stores the
Ford dealership the
Farm implements dealership the
Hardware store the bank
(Or ex-bank I no longer
Remember which) and the
Wagon Wheel Café where
We were about to eat and
Up on the hill
Slight hill
Rising above town toward the
Interstate on the ridge the
Mary Queen of Heaven
Brick church

1882—Holy sacrament of the Mass first
        Celebrated just east of this site

1883—Mary Queen of Heaven Parish was
        Established and a church erected on this site

1902—This present church erected and
        Blessed by the Bishop of Nesqually

1990—This church was placed on the
        National Register of Historic Places by the
        United States Department of the Interior

Church now appearing wellkept but
Not a showplace as we read the
Small glassed in bulletin board
Listing the weekly and
Monthly services
Two masses every
Sunday as I recall or
Perhaps there were
Two different times for
Masses depending upon
Which day of the month and
Standing with our backs to the
Church we could look down
Over the town the short
Blocks of one and two story
Brick buildings your
Quintessential classic
Small farm country town the
Likes of which you saw just
About every five miles in that
Open formerly prairie land
Five miles being just about the
Distance you could drive a horse and
Wagon into town on a Saturday for
Supplies and do your shopping and
(Equally important) gossiping at the
Hardware store or café and
Turn around and go
Home again in a day and
Perhaps more important
Five miles being the practical
Distance to haul your grain by team at
Harvest to the nearest
Elevator on the nearest
Granger railroad branch line
None of these towns came into
Being until the railroads for these were
Not subsistence farms suited to
Growing or raising a
Little of everything that
Could keep you alive these farms
This land was monoculture

Commercial farming and without the
Railroad to bring your supplies in and
Your harvest out there was
Nothing you could do out there on those
Vast former prairies now
Oceans of wheat where the
Railroads in the late 1870s and
Early 1880s brought thousands and
Thousands of immigrant mostly
Scandinavian and German
Families
Peasants but often smart
Educated often Lutheran peasants
Land hungry you could only
Subdivide those family lots so many
Times in crowded Europe and
Imagine
Just imagine
What a windfall the
Thought of *hundreds* of acres
Must have been so they came and
Endured
In some places
Bitter winters that
No one had told them about and
Hotter summers than *anyone* ever
Imagined but being smart and tough and
Hardworking they built those farms and
Now their descendents the
Lucky ones rode across those
Same fields in $100,000 two story
Cab fully enclosed and air conditioned
Combines that if they owned the
Land outright they could probably
Afford and if they didn't the
Debt for those huge complex machines
Might just drive them
Under
Not our problem
Not immediately as we
Wondered at the messages
Written in wheat by the

Wind and
Tell you the truth I
Don't even remember anymore
We went everyplace almost at least
Twice so *were* they harvesting
Wheat in mid-summer I
Distinctly remember the
Golden color or
Well
No matter
Prose is linear
Poetry circular you
Read it then if it's
Any good you
Read it again and the
Emotion comes back
Too
You keep coming back as we
Kept going back
Most people
You'd think
Would only need to drive from
Minneapolis to Seattle once but
Not us
Oh no
We did it at
Least a couple times feeling
Each time that we
Must have missed or
Not understood or
Failed to appreciate
Something in that almost
Endless prairie of the
Upper Midwest (Dakotas, Eastern
Montana) and then after a few
Mountain ranges the
Huge dry and mostly flat
Prairie of eastern Oregon and
Washington State that do not often
Appear featured in the travel
Brochures
In retrospect I

Suppose what I didn't
Get because it was simply
Outside my experience was the
The rhythm the reality of
Agricultural life where what
Happened on the farms those
Family farms that was
What mattered and the towns
Though essential were
Not the heart of those
Places so we
Would sail those oceans of
Wheat those inland
Seas of corn
Time and again but
Always remain
Ignorant of the
Language or
Languages in
Which those
Messages
Blowing across those
Golden fields
Were
Written

And we were there
Listening to Saint
Mary whispering
Some kind of
Prayer or
Prophecy
In
The
Wind

Pray for me
St. Mary

Pray for me
St. Mary

Pray for me
St. Mary

For I
Know not

What

I

Do.

Between Them

All those Charlie Russell
Paintings where the sun slants in
Low over the mountains and/or
Plains and everything glints
Orange and purple
Artistic license I always thought
But no it's
Really like that and as
Cowboy poet
(Before they called them
Cowboy poets)
Powder River Jack Lee
Once (sorta) put it:
You don't know about skies
Until you have seen them
With their blues and their reds
And fair purples
Between them
Powder River Jack Lee
Claimed he once rode for
Buffalo Bill Cody way back when
Then became a singing cowboy
When they came into
Fashion and travelled the
Southwest with his wife
(Another Cody graduate)
Playing wherever
Don't know that he
Ever made it big but you
Know he did have a
Way with words and now
Standing on the
Side of Boot Hill above
Virginia City, Montana yes
Named for Virginia City,
Nevada by some hopefuls well
VC, Montana never made it
Anywhere near as big as
VC Nevada did but
Big enough to have become the

State capitol temporarily when the
Rest of the state was grizzly bears and
Sagebrush
Alder Gulch they called it
Initially
Which we saw
The alders still there
The gulch still there
Down by the river
Where they found all that
Alluvial
That is to say
In the river bank washed
Down from elsewhere
Gold all you had to do was
Dig it out of the frigid water and the
People who got rich and stayed rich
Supplied the miners with their
Necessities or
Like Henry Plummer
Sheriff but also murderous
Robber whose gang was
Finally eliminated by the
Committee of vigilantes
And the last five or worst five or
Maybe the most convenient five
Strung up right there in
Virginia City down there where the
Shadows fell now and buried for
Safekeeping up here on
Boot Hill overlooking the
City itself
City out west being not a
Descriptive but a
Hopeful word there were
Cities out west consisting of a
General store at a
Lonesome crossroads you
Called it a city and hoped
People who didn't know better
Which was almost everybody
Back then

Would flock to your new
Municipality where (with useful
Forethought) you may have claimed and
Staked out lots which the
Newcomers would buy and
Thereby turn your vison
(Also your investment) into a
Reality
So Alder Gulch did boom for awhile until they
Took out all the gold and
Eliminated the bad guys by means of a
Citizens Uplift Society
AKA necktie party and
Then of course once the gold was
Gone the majority of the citizens
Who had not got rich
Moved on to Helena
Or wherever and
Did it all over again
Leaving behind the
Shabby pretentious architecture of
Sudden wealth where men had
Lived in tents and waded in
Snowmelt water among the
Alders trying to
Get in
Get Rich and
Get Out in the
Undying creed of the
Then new
Now old
West where no one
Almost no one
Built for posterity and
Anyway if you did get
Rich where in the world would you
Stay out there in the middle of
Just about nowhere
In a gulch
It was a gulch
Dark in the shadows now at
Sundown

Dark between the two ridges
Dark down there where they got
Hung but up here on the
Side of Boot Hill
They got small white
Gravestones
All in a row
Jack Gallagher
Hayes Lyons
Frank Parish
Boone Helm
George Lane
Up there in the sunlight
Late afternoon golden
Sunlight with the
Sky off to the west
Those clouds
Sun behind them
With their

Blues

And their

Reds and

Fair

Purples

Between

Them.

Deadstick

Deadstick as the
Bartender at one of the
Many many many
Saloons bars casinos
Full of gambling machinery
Chrome blinking lights video and
Noisy and the old folks
Toddling along the sidewalks
Clutching their styrofoam
Cups of quarters
Very historic and a
Vision of hell if you know or
Could imagine what the
Place had been like just a
Few years before
Avant le deluge
Before the state legislature
Gave the good or perhaps
Not so good citizens of
Deadwood, South Dakota
Permission to sell their
Town down the river
Sell out
For that's what it would
Mean
Their entire community
You can't afford the taxes once
Gambling comes in and
Everyplace appreciates 10 or 20 times
What it was before you could
Put one-armed bandits in every
Piece of real estate
All the buildings with their
Original facades
Sop to the preservationists
But bulldozers and backhoes behind those
Facades didn't just *gut* them they
Tore them right down and in their
Place put modern buildings ideal for
Housing large heavy and hungry for

Electricity gambling machinery
Modern plumbing and
All the rest so that a
Town that had been
Preserved in
Well
Call it amber or
Maybe dust and rust and
Neglect but a
Town that had once in itself
Been a complete museum
Piece became a shell
Less than a
Shell of its former self
And no one in town
No one who *was* in town
Still owned any piece of it
Unless thay knew how and were
Willing to run a gambling
Casino

But we wandered around
Anyway having gone to the
Trouble of driving there
Looked in to the ex saloon now
Casino where
James Butler Hickock
A/k/a
Wild Bill one PM
Sat
Against his custom
With his
Back
Facing the door and some
Low life who resented all the
Innocent and uninnocent men
Bill had killed
Walked into the joint and
Walked up to him and
Drew a gun and
Shot him in the head
(Or was it the back) from

Behind
Which may have been just as
Well for Wild Bill whose
Eyesight
Once extraordinary had
Begun failing him
(Possibly a complication of
Venereal disease) and was
Certainly just as well in fact
Wonderful for western lore and
Legend what more could you
Ask for than a notorious
Gunslinger dying with his
Boots on in a
Saloon with his
Back to the door and
Holding only
Eights and aces which
Promptly or
Eventually became
Known as the
Dead
Man's
Hand

So we wandered
Along the once-historic
Streets of what had until
Recently been a near-perfectly
Preserved late nineteenth
Century western
Mining town and didn't see
Much that really interested us
Until we came upon
Stumbled upon a store
Façade like all the
Rest
Pure Victorian the
Tall plate glass windows
But inside

Far as we could see
Pure late nineteenth century
Hardware store full of
Wooden shelves and bins and
Implements and ancient
Advertisements and
Manufacturers' calenders all the
Impedimentia of late
Nineteenth early 20th century
Retailing and wholesaling of
Everything you could
Or might once have
Needed for
Mining and a small
Handlettered white
Sign taped to one of the
Front windows read

This property is
Not for sale
Don't even
Dream of
It

And inside
Quite near the
Entrance a
Visitors' book
Full of names
To which we added
Ours and further
Inside seated in a
Comfortable armchair
Agnes Ayres
Wife of
Albro Ayres whose family had
Owned Ayres Hardware in
Downtown Deadwood
South Dakota since 1876 who said
They've all sold out and
Now there's no grocery store no
Clothing store no furniture

Store no car dealership and
I'm one of the
Last five that's
Left

And I wondered why it was
That in looking for
Signs and portents or
Some kind of prophecy or
Message I would
Find that the only
Words I
Sort of
Understood would be
Scrawled on a
Handwritten sheet and
Taped to an ancient
Hardware store
Front window by a
Seventy six year old
Widow in

Deadstick

South

Dakota.

Shot-To-Pieces

Wind shook the knotted
Fringes on the little leather
Drum
Sacred drum so the kid who
Sold it to me said
Buffalo skull in white
Paint on the brown
Leather
No one else around
Just us and the kid who
Wheeled up to us as we
Stood by the cemetery
Full of graves of the
Massacre some
One hundred years
Earlier but quite
Vivid and immediate to the
Sioux who were
Stuck on that reservation
Their land and who knows
Maybe fine for summer but
They were a nomadic people and I
Have to believe would have spent
Winters someplace less
Exposed than those grasslands in
South Dakota with the
Steep ridge among the
Grasslands with just
Enough elevation and
Hence moisture to maintain
Pines along the top and
Upper flanks
Hence the
Name

Those long leather thongs like
Buffalo ponies tails
Whipping up from the
Bottom of the drum and

Beating upon the taut
Leather
Sending some
Message
I knew not
What and
Doubt that the
Kid with his ten-speed and
Miracle fiber carrying
Bag had any idea
Either
The eagle feathers and
Little bags of tobacco
Tied to the graves and to the
Fence around the graves on
Top of the small ridge by the
Chapel I
Forget which
Denomination
Overlooking the site of the
Massacre
Wounded Knee
Two hundred unarmed
Sioux gunned down by the
U.S. Army after
Some jumpy Sioux or
Soldier got nervous and then the
Wounded Knee reoccupation
Some 85 or so years later the
Militants versus the Feds in
Awful recapitulation
Kid said he saw
Part of it
Burning houses then his
Mother sent him away to live with
Relatives off the reservation
Until it was all (at least the
Shooting part of it) over
You need only ride around that
Reservation
The unmarked roads
Unmarked houses

Don't be there
After dark
People don't leave their
Houses unguarded
Someone is always there
Someone always keeping an eye
The bitterness runs
Deep
And they're warriors they
Don't know what to do with
Themselves except
Fight a
Friend who's
Part Sioux and
Danced the
Sun Dance three times and has the
Scars on his back and
Chest to
Prove it tells me

We stand there
Talking with the kid who
Charged us $20 for the drum
Back when $20 seemed like
More than it does now
But I thought
So what
That's $.07 for
Every man woman and
Child
Buried on that
Ridge including
The kid's aunt
Ann Respects Nothing

So I asked the
Kid his name

Lawrence Shot

Is that Lakota?

No it's short for

Shot-

To-

Pieces.

Want To Know

There it was the
Billboard sign over the
Crest of the rise on a
Little rise of ground itself
Above the trailer above the small
Store with the permanent
Awning extending over the
Gaspumps about
Sixty miles in any
Direction from the
Nearest anywhere and unlike
So many other signs or
Messages this one was real
Clear in its ambiguity:

Loma Alta
Pop. ?

So we
Naturally
Parked a little ways away from the
Store since we didn't
Need gas or in fact
Need anything we could
Think of except to find out a
Little bit more about

Loma Alta
Pop. ?

Which had appeared on our
Rand McNally road atlas
South section of Texas page as a
Small black dot on a
Thin red line south of the
Hill country and
West of Austin on a
Two lane highway
Connecting the
Hill country

(Which was itself
Not overpopulated) with
Del Rio
Nearest real city right there on the
Rio Grande river that is to say the
Border

And walked from the car in that
South Texas midsummer heat
Every step feeling as if the
Sun itself would push us down into the
Dirt parking lot
Such as it was
Never felt heat quite as
Hard it seemed as
That before
And then the relief—a weight
Lifted—of the shade the
Oldfashioned country store
Gas and groceries sort of place
Where these days
No doubt
You bought the things you had
Run out of between runs to the
Big city
Just plain wooden shelves with
Canned and packaged goods and a
Couple coolers for
Pop and beer and
Whatnot and a
Small card table with
Mostly old but a few new
Chairs and seated at them with
Chairs to spare the
Owner
T.L. Zorn and his wife
Doris
Who talked more
Though they were both
Friendly and a
Weatherbeaten local rancher who'd been
Interviewed by James Michener for his

Big *Michener*-style novel about
Texas
(Michener almost always did those
Michener-style books) and
When the rancher took his
Stetson off you saw a
Deep crease from the band mark and
Almost white skin on his
Forehead
Gray hair
Decent guy it seemed
Not the local big man about whom he
Told some well-worn stories to
All their sorrow the
Oil rigs just hadn't
Drifted quite down their way and it
Struck me how *drift* was the
Western word
Word of those great plains
Where weather people animals
Even oil
Drifted
Even as she and I
Drifted or tried to
Drift and
Slowly in the air-conditioned
Little store sitting at the
Table with T.L. and Doris Zorn
We gradually felt a
Return to something like
Normal
Normal temperature for us
Anyway and I asked about

Pop. ?

Usually it's 2
Just us
Doris replied
But when one of the kids is
Here—I've got a

Daughter in college
I think she said
So we just leave it
Question mark and
People drifting by
Come in because they

Want

To

Know.

Home

The dry heat
The arid landscape
Just on the other side of that
Windshield from us as we
Ran off the miles
The long miles
Between towns
Thought we knew
Something about
Distances out west
But no
We knew *nothing until we*
Hit West Texas and
Suddenly you went from
Not 50 or 100 but
Two hundred fifty miles
Between towns of any
Size
Down there by the
Border but not the
Border where most
People were crossing because
There was
Nothing
Absolutely nothing to
Support life as most of us
Knew it
Down
There

Scared me some if you
Want to know the truth
Even though we were
Right there on the
Interstate
Interstate 10
With cars or trucks
Passing at semi-frequent
Intervals *I*
Kept thinking

What if?
All relative I know
Friends come from
Back east and we
Take them out onto the
Prairie
Minnesota prairie
Midwinter say and
They look at that
Vast expanse of
White far as the eye can see
And
Though they're
Actually farms within
View they say
(Especially if it's
Overcast)
They say:
Grimmesota
Or they don't come at all
My parents her parents my
Sister her sister all but
One uncle
The uncle who lives out
West in Colorado
Rest of em have *never*
Ever come out west to
Visit us and my guess is
They
Never
Ever
Will

Not bitter about this you
Understand it's just a matter of
Perspective they were
Brought up to believe that
Boston
Of all places is the
Epicenter of the universe
Harvard
M.I.T.

Durgin-Park and so on
And to leave is simply to
Voluntarily depart from the
Promised land much like the
Native Americans who having been
Presented with the facts of
Theology (Bible, Mass, Alcohol
Long pants)
Nevertheless persisted in their
Heathenism and therefore
Deserved
Deserved
Whatever they got or
More specifically
Didn't get as a
Consequence
In leaving our lives became
Unimaginable to them and
There we were
Some 100
Some 200
Some 250
Miles from Del Rio
Which in my new retrospect
Looked pretty *sivilized* as
Huck Finn would have put it
To me now and taking in all that
Vast (to us) emptiness that
World of unending aridity emptiness and
Distance only the
Blessed Interstate to
Connect us with
Anything we knew and
Any possibility of
Survival and
As we drove
We got
Hungrier and hungrier
Until finally we saw an
Exit marked for
Kent, Texas on the map
Which looked precisely like a

Crossroads in the middle of
Absolutely nowhere with one
Weatherbeaten old wooden white-painted
False fronted oldfashioned
General store and we
Pulled up alongside where a
Few other cars
Mostly dusty local
Pickups were
Pulled up alongside and we
Went in and the store
Manager in big black stetson and
Deeply tanned face and
Unbelievably tough hands was
Rattling off Spanish to
One of the customers as we
Politely waited our turn in the
Blessed dark and shade amid the
Old wooden shelves full of
Pretty much every
Necessity of life and
Ranching until he was done
And we inquired about the
Vacuum wrapped in clear
Plastic baloney sandwiches that he
Had in his cooler
Come in fresh
Every week I
Have one for
Lunch every
Day
Which was
Good enough for us and
Outside
Sitting in that
Heat with the
Car doors open we
Unwrapped the plastic
From those sandwiches and
I notice
We notice the
Self-adhesive paper

Label on the front
Which read
Deli Express
Eden Prairie
Minnesota
About ten miles from
Where we lived and
Which I took as a
Sign that

The further you
Go away the

Closer

You are

To

Home.

Mission

Almost suppertime
By the time we
Reached Las Cruces, New Mexico
And then drove nearly
Through it missing nearly
All the exits so we had to
Stop and turn around and
Return to Exit 3 where a
Strip mall and a couple
Picturesque anchor stores and the
Usual winding and tree shaded
Access roads lured us to
Yet another McDonald's where on the
Front lawn and in the
Shade of the sign with the
Golden arches a vagrant
Perhaps my age
Sat mugging with his
Dog some kind of
Shepherd and something else
Mix
How bad can I be
If my dog loves me
May have been the message
Along with his cardboard sign:
Work Wanted

Not hardly was the opinion of the
Upper class vagrant with neatly
Arranged if dirty pack and
Sitting inside in the air-conditioning with
Multiple cups of coffee in
Front of him
Admission tickets as it were to
This the local
Clean well lighted place
Ernest Hemingway's famous
Formula for *someplace* in which to
Seek refuge from the

Nada

Well I could easily
See myself in that
No longer so young
Man's place sitting there at that
Little table with the preformed plastic
Bench along the wall and the
Little swiveling chair on the
Other side of the table
So I asked the no longer so
Young man if we could
Join him and said we were
Going to have some supper and wondered if
He was willing to tell us a
Little about life on the road
Would he be interested in
Joining us as our guest for
Supper

Took him a minute to
Understand the offer then he
Understood and the three of us
Waited in line there were
No waiters at this
Café so we waited in
Line and then placed our
Orders
Have anything you want
I told him
We're having quarter
Pounders with cheese

That's OK?

That's OK

I assured him so we all ordered
Quarter pounders with cheese and
Returned to the table and
While we ate our
Cheeseburgers I asked him about

Life on the road
Which had once been
When he was young
Perhaps good-looking and
Young and
New Mexico was a
Very different place then
You could stop by any
Farm and ask if they had
Work and you'd work for
Them for a few days or a
Week and they'd give you
Someplace to spread your
Sleeping bag but
Now it was all changed and you
Ended up sleeping under
Highway bridges with the
Sand blowing into your
Sleeping bag and no one or
Almost no one wanted to
Hire a middle aged no longer
So young or so
Good looking man with a
Ragged pack on his
Back and no
Fixed
Address

We talked for a little while and I
Tried to understand where or how he'd
Become separated from his
Family mother remarried
Stepfather when he was about 17 and he
Thought he had his sister's address
But he didn't want to
Get back in touch until he
Had a little more to
Show for
Himself

And where will you sleep tonight?

Probably under a
Bridge it's a
Six mile walk
Across

Town

To the

Mission.

Roadrunner

Roadrunner
Roadrunner
Scampering across the road and
Over the ditch and
Into the brush
Materialized then
Dematerialized
Before our eyes
Early morning
Baja Rio Grande valley
Soon chili farms on
Either side
Bright green against the
Tans and grays and
Mauves between them of the
Dry ridges cutting a line
Across the blue sky
Then:
Hatch, New Mexico
Chili Capital of the World
And home of the
Annual chili festival
To which we would have
Happily invited ourselves
Had we been there at the
Right time of year
Which we weren't
Chilies bright green in those
Flat irrigated fields
Rio Grande's snowmelt
Water run out of the
High San Juans and
Tributary Rio Chama and
Down through Barranca Hill
Past Embudo
Past Velarde
Where I knew or
Thought I knew
Someone and
South through

Albuquerque through
Socorro and past
Truth Or Consequences
(Formerly Hot Springs) into this
Lower Rio Grande valley of
New Mexico
Gentler hills
Broad flat fields for
Growing chilies
All kinds of chilies from
Some you could eat to
Some you couldn't
Depending upon what
You were used to or
Weren't depending upon
Where you grew up and
What they fed you
You grow up where they
Grow cows you get
Dairy based bland
All that milk and butter from
Cows residing all winter in
Warm barns in cold
Climates

Air so pure in that
Rio Grande valley that it
Seemed like mountain water
Clear pure transparent the
Beauty of knowing
Not a damn thing or
Almost not a damn thing about
Where you were
Didn't speak Spanish
Hardly anymore
You know they don't
Talk about it much elsewhere
But in New Mexico the
Outsiders are called
Anglos
You Chinese Native American
Jewish Whatever you're an

Anglo while the natives of
New Mexico they're
Hispanic and their
Attitude is very
Simple:
We were here before
You arrived and we'll
Still be here after
You're
Gone
Quiet unassuming gentle gracious
Many of them some
Lowriders excluded
But cross them and
You might well find
Yourself
Gone

That story about the Los Alamos
Scientists on a hunting trip
Crossed a couple locals and
By the time the law got around to
Investigating their
Disappearance the
Scene of the crime
So to speak had been
Reconfigured with a
Borrowed county
Bulldozer
You thought you saw that
Roadrunner well
Maybe you did and
Maybe you
Didn't

But
As we were saying:
Hatch, New Mexico
Chili Capital of the
World
Whether the rest of the
World knew or cared or

Not
And entering town we
Passed the growers' sheds and
More fields and signs for
Warehouses
Not large warehouses
Chilies aren't that
Big you know they
Just pack a
Wallop

And then into town
Itself just a few blocks of
Mostly one story stores
Quiet
Shadows cool and
Blue
Was it Monet who
Noticed that
Shadows were
Blue
Main road the
Two lane becomes
Main Street which is the
Only way you keep a
Small town downtown
Alive and we're
Looking for
Someplace to eat
Breakfast
(Forgive me Dear Reader if
This poem sometimes seems an
Odyssey of *Places We Ate*)
Because
Well
If you're driving through and
Looking for you
Know not what the
One thing you
Usually do know at
Regular intervals is
That you are

Hungry

Couple possibilities in the
Café department
Some in the shadows some
Facing the sun but
Awfully hard to
Know just as a
Couple *Anglo* strangers
Driving through so we
Stop in the local
Police Department knowing that
Cops usually don't want to
Give themselves food
Poisoning and ask
And the lady behind the
Counter (Hispanic like
Almost everyone else we
Saw) tells us
The Hatch Café
We eat there
All the time
Right down the
Street

And what's good enough for the
Boys and girls in blue is
Certainly good enough for
Us so we repair to the
Hatch Café which is on the
Sunny side of the street
Warm sunshine pouring in those
Tall plate glass windows of some
Formerly probably late nineteenth
Early twentieth century retail
Establishment but now all that
Once varnished woodwork
Covered with a layer of
All purpose white paint
Morning warm sunlight on
White paint and an
Old linoleum floor

(As I recall) with the
Original oak no doubt
Still beneath it and a
Mismatched assortment of
Chrome and formica
1950s furniture that
Never had a chance to
Become retro
Chic

Because Hatch is still Hatch in its
Old way of being Hatch where
As it turns out an
Elderly
Well
Elderly to us
Then
Not quite so
Elderly to us
Now couple
Frank and
Shirley
Were riding out their
Lease with a
Restaurant that
Probably wasn't making them a
Whole lot of money
Grand plan?
Fond scheme?
Dumb Luck?
Bad Luck?
Hey we're not
Young
To be
Doing what they were
Doing every morning all that
Up early
Day after
Day

But the breakfast as the
Lady in blue promised was

Delicious
Eggs over sunny on
White plates and a
Side bowl of green
Chili
Made there from
Local chilies
And a sign by the
Cash register
Handlettered sign that
Read:

No Credit unless
You are over
Eighty and have
Both parents
Still
Living

And somewhere
Maybe written with a
Finger on the
Transparent plate glass
Gleaming in the
Sun I also
Read:

We were here before
You arrived and we'll
Still be here after
You're
Gone

Chilies aren't that
Big you know they
Just pack a
Wallop

You thought you saw that
Roadrunner well
Maybe you did and
Maybe you

Didn't

Roadrunner

Roadrunner.

River

Black crosses against the
Sky on the canyon ridges
Above the
Alta Rio Grande
River valley the
Canyon walls closer in
Now you could
Spend afternoons or
Mornings in shadow
Depending on what
Side of the
Canyon you lived on
If you lived there
If you were
Living at all as the
People for whom those
Crosses were mounted were
Not any longer though they
Could not have been
More alive in spirit for the
People who remembered and
Memorialized and
Sanctified their
Deaths with those
Crosses

And no I didn't
Think then that those
Crosses rose there in
Memory of anyone I
Knew I
We
Hardly knew anyone
In fact knew just about
No one in that
Upper Rio Grande valley
Just one person or there had
Been just one person until
Night before speaking at a
Public telephone in the

Hotel La Fonda lobby
(Forgive the repetition
La Fonda means
Hotel)
Anyway the swanky
Downtown plaza center of
Old Santa Fe courtyard of
La Fonda there I was
Standing at a
Public telephone amid the
Swanky shops selling
Very nice and
Very overpriced
(To us anyway)
Tourist merchandise the
Turquoise the
Navajo blankets the
Pueblo pottery and you
Get the idea
Amid all that there I was
Trying to reach
Marshall Rigsby whom I had
Last spoken to in
Bangkok, Thailand when he was
There on a mission of
Self-recovery and I was
Trying to make some
Sense of Southeast Asia
Close as I could
Get at that time to
Vietnam
Where I never went
Or wanted to go but where
All of us went
Somehow
Which is not the same as
Saying all of us stood in
Paddies up to our armpits while
Shrapnel or tracer bullets
Friendly or otherwise
Rained down

We met at the *Big M*
Hotel Malaysia
Former R&R hotel for
American military turned into a
Run down never maintained
El cheapo tourist and hippie
Traveler hotel catering to
Wandering young people and
Transient low budget
New Zealanders and so on
Hotel Malaysia in
Faded plastic letters up the
Side of the building and
Black scum lined empty
Swimming pool in the
Courtyard and sleek small
Courteous Thai
Pimps with the always
Beautiful and often
Very young Thai
Prostitutes on their arms
Led to their customers
Often German sex tourists in by the
Planeload for the world's most
Beautiful and cheapest
Women
You want
One guy says to me as we're
Standing in the creaky
Uncleaned elevator and
He has an exquisite woman all in
Diaphanous white on his arm
No
I replied
Only partly true
Who
If not married
Wouldn't

Anyway
As I began to
Say I

Met Marshall Rigsby there
Marshall alive to other
Possibilities and
Searching for
Searching for
Well in the course of a
Long evening and many
Many Tiger brand beers I
Think I understood
Something of what he
Sought
Sought solace
Sought peace
Sought some kind of
Redemption after his
Wife was gunned down by a
Drifter
Psychotic it
Turned out who
Marshall had brought home from a
Rainbow Tribe festival
Do the guy a favor
Give him some work on their
Ranch as he called it on the
Banks of the Alta Rio Grande in
Velarde, New Mexcio
Marshall wrote it
Carefully for me in my
Notebook when we parted the
Next morning after having
Closed down first the
Bar at the *Big M* and then the
Bar at the
Now I can't remember
Place across the street
Where the whores there
Also would have gladly
Diverted us but for
Some reason
We
Kept
Talking

Two not quite
Lost souls but
Searching for
Something and Marshall had his
Old girlfriend still friend
Some kind of artist
Chinese-Canadian woman whom I met
Briefly when she
Came downstairs to
Find out what in hell was
Keeping them but he
Never did get specific
About their present
Relationship and
Maybe they
Didn't know it
Themselves
He'd bought $1500 worth of
Rubies in Hong Kong where he'd
Met or travelled to or
I don't know what with her
And then to Bangkok where he
Talked about travelling on to
India
Do work for
Mother Teresa
While she
While she
I don't know what and I'm
Not sure he knew or
Maybe not even she
Knew either

Talked almost all that night
Two refugees from
Family
Marshall felt
Unloved and
So did I
Difference is I was
Not burdened by almost
Unbearable grief over the

Death of a wife
May God forbid
My wife was home
Safe and sound and
Waiting for me to
Return with
We hoped
Some kind of story or
Insight worth
Writing
While Marshall had left his
Ranch and his brother and his
Mother (father former
Los Alamos scientist as I
Understood it having
Passed away) and
Marshall said the rubies were for
Custom jewelry and and
Pool cues and saddle hardware he
Made but there was
Inherited money
Inherited land
Trust of some kind as I
Gathered and
None of that
Obviously
Made his
Life
Worth
Living

So we talked till late
Two older brothers
Understood
That much about
Each other and the
Distance from
Family and
Buddhism and
Well
There we were
And before we

Parted he wrote out his
Name and address and the
Radio relay telephone number
(No cellphones back then) and said
If you're ever in
New Mexico
Give me a
Call

So I did
That evening before and
Before the static on the
Radiophone line
Killed all meaning I
Understood the
Woman who answered the
Phone to say
Marshall is dead

Tried calling
Back but
Static
Static
Static

Could have just
Forgotten about the whole
Thing but
Something
Something in the
Way that unknown
Woman on the other
End of the line said
Marshall is dead
Haunted me
No *Marshall died from*
Just
Marshall is dead

Thought about it
Overnight and the
Next morning we

Decided to drive up to
Velarde, New Mexico on the
Alta Rio Grande
Which we did and the
Little orchards in the
Narrow flood plain between the
Canyon walls grew green against the
Tans and the grays and the
Purples between them
Yes you've seen those
Same colors before in
Georgia O'Keefe
Landscapes among
Other places and
Finally stopped at one
Small orchard roadside
Stand and the woman there
Eastern european name
Said yes
We'd just passed the road for the
Rigsby place and we could
Park right there in the
Shade of her trees if we
Wanted to because the
Dirt road into the
Little ranch was
Rough

So we did
Walked back in that
Dry hot sun and
Under that blue blue sky
Beneath those black
Black crosses and I
Carried a big stick
(Everybody seemed to have
At least one large dog) and
At a small cabin
David Rigsby
Marshall's brother
Opened the door and
Invited us in

And as it happened the
Family had just
Celebrated rites for the
Anniversary of Marshall's
Mysterious death and
Disappearance some
Five years before
Died in Calcutta
Suicide
So the Chinese woman
Told them and she
Claimed she
Wasn't there
Had not
Been in Bangkok
But I saw her
Met her
I told him
She returned a few
Rubies and papers
Said Marshall was
Cremated beside the
Ganges in
Benares and his
Ashes floated on a
Leaf

Down

The

River.

Rain

Rain
Rain running down the
Adobe walls of the
Sagebrush Inn
Real adobe
Inn originally called
Something like
Las Vigas
No they're the heavy roof beams
La Chamisa
Originally called I think the
Chamisa Inn then changed to
Sagebrush because the
Tourists
Including us
Had no idea what
Chamisa is
But it was real adobe
Built I think during the
Depression and later
Georgia O'Keefe who
Gave this part of the
World its visual
Identity
Back east
That is
Southwesterners had
No doubt who they were or
What they looked like
Cowboys knew what cowboys
Looked like from
Reading dime novels and
Seeing horse operas and
Pueblos darn well
Blue jeans bright shirts
Shawls and so on
Braided hair
Hispanics
Well
They too had put their

Mark on the look of the
Land
The adobes following the
Pueblos
Adobe a mixture of straw and
Clay
Mud in other
Words and you dried it in the
Sun to harden it and then
Piled the blocks one atop the
Next for a building that was in
Some ways indistinguishable
From the landscape
Franciscan padres made
Missions out of it
(What else was there
Timber was scarce
Quarrying stone out of the
Question)
Actually
The *Indians* recruited or impressed or
Converted and baptized *by* the
Franciscan padres made
Missions out of it
Hewed the *vigas* in the
Mountains and brought them down and
Out of that mixture of
Franciscan piety and
Local craft and
Ancient tradition there
Rose the adobe missions that with
Every rain lost a little of their
Substance and had to be at
Regular intervals
Rebuilt again

After this rain for
Instance we could see the
Rivulets cutting into the
Lower courses
Actually the smooth outer
Coating of adobe applied over the

Lower courses and running off
Muddy water
Earth returned to
Earth again
No danger here for this
Little chapel in its own
Quiet plaza off the
Main road just south of
Taos, New Mexico at a
Place now and for a
Long time known as
Ranchos de Taos
For this place was
Famous
Painted by O'Keefe
Photographed by Adams and
Porter and since then by
Just about everyone
Else

But not today
Not with all this rain
Rain washing down the
Outside of the church and
Rain washing over the low wall
Enclosing the graveyard in front of the
Church and rain soaking into the
Dirt plaza itself
No dust today and
Rain soaking into our
Levi's jackets
Old Levi's jackets
Not prewashed or
Stonewashed or
Abraded by the
Manufacturer with pumice
Just worn soft and
Weathered not unlike the
Mission adobe and our
Hair not yet turned gray
Not unlike the dye all
Bleached out and back to

White cotton of the jackets
But getting there
Soon a
Few years
We were that age
Youth over and
What did I
Have to show for it
Not much
Certainly not much in the
Conventional sense no
Grand titles or even
Small titles and
No money to speak of
Trading their hours
For that handful of
Dimes
So sure they'd make it
Baby in their
Prime
Except
Physically
Prime was soon to be
Soon to be
Say
Another five years
Over
And yet

And yet
Like the

Adobe

With

Every

Rain.

Sabine Women

Pulled into Taos, New Mexico
Needing a shower
Not such a great thing to
Need when you find yourself in a
Tourist town at the height of the
Tourist season
No
That was
Some other time this
Time we already had
That room at the
Sagebrush just
Outside of town and we'd
Driven into town just to
Look around before
Supper
Beautiful place though
The adobe
Plaza with low shade trees
Benches and so on
Parking
Even found a
Parking spot
Guess it was just
Meant to be the
Parking spot and
La Fonda de Taos
Not to be confused with
La Fonda de Santa Fe
Although that might have been the
Hope on the part of
La Fonda da Taos which was
As you quickly saw inside the
Dark shady tall ceilinged old
Woodwork lobby with the
Mezzanine above as
You quickly saw
But you immediately
Saw also that the
Place was unique

Big paintings and the
Old woodwork
Patina of age and character
Behind all that
You just weren't
Quite sure *what*
Character and then you
Noticed the guy at the desk
Somewhere in that late middle age
Where people can and do
Get lost between working and
Not working and between
Settled comfort and
Settled or maybe
Unsettled poverty
This guy *not* in any kind of
Hotel uniform and looking
Wiry and tough yet not
Menacing
(You don't want your desk help
Looking menacing) and he says to
Her
Pretty lady what
Can I do for
You
And the funny thing was
You knew immediately he'd
Used that line a
Hundred or thousand
Times before and that he'd
Meant
Sincerely
Every single
One
And she asks about the
D.H. Lawrence Art Museum
Mentioned in a sign and with some
Yellowing news clipping about it
Displayed (was it) behind glass
Behind the desk counter
Pretty lady for
Anyone else it's $2

Admission unless you're a
Hotel guest but for
You this
Afternoon it's for
Free
And you had to
Hand it to him
Here was a not so tall
Late middle aged guy
Smoking a cigarette and with
Breathing tubes on a harness
Around his neck leading to his
Nostrils and trailing a little
Pressure tank of
Oxygen on little wheels
Behind him and he
Still had an eye and
Still had the moves
For the ladies
Hell I didn't feel
Threatened I
Admired the guy's style and
You had to think
If he's this good now
What must he have
Been like in his
Prime
Introduced ourselves
You're a long way from home
Which was true even if we
Weren't quite sure
Where was home and he was
John Chapman
Working for
Saki Karavas who owned
La Fonda but who was
Too busy every night
Squiring the girls so I
Just shine his shoes and
I've got me a little room
Upstairs by the
Ice machine and

Once a week my
Duster comes over from
Cimarron to
Dust
My
Room
As John put it as we
Followed him or more
Precisely his little white
Oxygen tank into Mr.
Saki's office behind the
Front counter where the oil
Paintings by the
Late
Great
English novelist were hung
Around the walls of the office
One titled
Rape of the Sabine Women and
Well
With all due
Respect Lawrence might just as well have
Stuck to literature with no
Excursions into pictorial art
But then
Hey
What did I know and
Hey
They were I
Believed authentic
And pictures of Saki with
Various celebrities not
Excluding Peter Fonda or
Was it Dennis Hopper from
Easy Rider days
(Did they film the
Commune scene somewhere
Around here I
Wondered)
And John left us alone in
There to commune with
Lawrence's ghost while he went

Back out front to
Man the desk and
Eventually we
Rejoined him and
Tipped him 5 dollars for his
Gracious hospitality and
John Chapman took a
Hit of oxygen and then a
Drag on his cigarette or
Maybe it was vice versa and I
Asked him
How he managed that
Very carefully he said *I*
Don't want to
Blow
Myself
Up
Asked John where he
Came from and at first he
Didn't really want to say then
Allowed it was
I think he said
Missouri where he and his
Wife had owned a
Restaurant until they
Came to a parting of the
Ways because she
Didn't like the way he was
Interviewing the
Waitresses
Which
Having already seen a
Small glimpse of
John Chapman in
Action I could just
Imagine

Next morning we're
Back in the plaza
Walking around after a
Lovely breakfast at the
Sagebrush and there's

John Chapman
Standing outside in the
Bright morning sun and
Morning cool air
Just outside
La Fonda de
Lawrence and
He's talking with a
Waitress
Young woman
Pretty woman
Obviously despite the
Disparity in ages
Quite taken with
John Chapman and
I think:
Good luck

All

You

Sabine

Women.

Belong

North through the
Kit Carson national forest
Quite a bit of forest
Really
You don't expect that much
Forest in New Mexico and of
Course it's low evergreen forest
Not some kind of overarching
Canopy that you might
Imagine if you came from
Elsewhere
In the southwest any
Trees at all were a
Big
Deal

You get to an open
Park that is
Meadow between the
Mountains but with their
Grass and artistically
Placed streams and clumps of
Trees and in this case three
Large rocks hence the
Name
Tres Piedras of course in that
Part of the world *tres*
Anything immediately
Suggests the
Trinity and in that part of the
World an intense
Literal
Brooding
Fatalistic and
Death and
Dying-centered
Variant of
Roman Catholicism
Originating with the
Spaniards but now of

Native stock and
Not without its
Admixture of the
Pre Christian
Ghosts
Witches
Spirits
Lies heavy upon the
Land in fact you might say
Rises up out of the land and
So flows through them
Mountain water
Mineral hot springs
Rio Grande river that you
Either are of there and
From there in that
Elemental way or
Being *anglo*
You just
Aren't

And if you *aren't* I
Suspect you're subject to
Spells of going just plain
Crazy what with all those
Unfamiliar familiars
Ghosts
Spirits
Witches the real but
Invisible world all around you and
When the *hantavirus* excitement
Began we skedaddled
I won't say where but
Call it a strategic or more
Candidly a panicked
Retreat
All they knew was
People's lungs were
Filling and smothering them in the
Space of very few hours and
Eventually they traced it to a
Korean origin a virus carried in

Dried mouse poop and urine that if
Say
You swept up while
Cleaning your house and you
Breathed it there was a
Very good chance you would
Die

No one else *left* of course
They stayed
There that was
Home but we left until
Over the weekend or in the
Next few days the scientists
Figured out why people were
Dying and then we
Came
Back
Resolved to avoid
Dusty places where
Mice might have
Been

Which certainly seemed not to include this
Classic late 1940s I would
Guess *Valentine* (the
Maker) diner sitting at the
Crossroads of New Mexico
Routes US 64 and 285
Take 64 east across the meadows and up
Into the
Sagebrush the
Chamisa and you
Reached Taos
Go west and you were
Headed toward the
Heart the most
Removed and almost
Secret part of
Hispanic New Mexico
Place where even the
Church itself had but a

Tenuous hold upon the
Ritual practiced in its
Name a place where the
Penitentes still
Reenacted the
Crucifixion every
Good Friday while the
Church looked on from
Afar at this
Rope and cross
Rather than
Nail and
Cross
Devotional act and was
Not sure if
They were
Going
Too
Far

You still saw in the
Distance usually
Away from the
Road the penitente
Moradas as their
Chapels their
Places of worship
Apart from the
Ordinary bishopric-
Sanctioned churches and
Missions these *moradas* were
Indigenous and you
Could not help but
Wonder if the
Sacrifice on the cross
Perpetuated the dark
Memory of mayan
Blood sacrifice for the
Peoples
This people
Partly of that
Central American corn

Culture and part
Probably
North american
Native american and
Part
Large part
Hispanic from when those
Tough fearless god driven
Franciscan padres walked and
Rode the earth looking for
Souls to convert and a
Land route to the
Pacific to the
Mission of
California

Dream
Vision
Devotion
Not the dust and chamisa and
Cacti that
Kept *them* going and
Bestowed a faith upon the
Land in the persons of those
Hispanic settlers who
Followed them who
Made it
Their
Own

Rites a
Little too colorful for the
Church much less the
Tourists and in this
Country the
Anglos
Well
Few and far between but a
Couple families evidently
Alive and well in
Tres Piedras, New Mexico
Tiny crossroads

Settlement with a
School and a garage and a
Few county offices and the
Rotting old yellow wooden
Water tower of the long-vanished
Denver and Rio Grande
Narrow gauge railroad branch to
Santa Fe from Antonito once
Known as the *Chili Line and*
Standing proudly in the
Morning sunlight on a
Slight rise of ground
Overlooking Tres Piedras
Including the
Tres piedras
Stood a perfect 1940s-something
Valentine (Mfg Co) diner made in
Wichita, Kansas and dragged out to the
Hinterlands of northern
Mountain New Mexico a piece of
Quintessential northeastern
Urban popular culture the
Stainless steel the
Deco details and the
Homemade wooden extension
(Original Valentines never
Sat more than
Ten people) and we
Returned from hantavirus
Recusement and
Somewhat spooked
We would always be somewhat
Spooked by the
Witches
Ghosts
Spirits we
Felt our spirits
Lift as we beheld this
Piece of what we knew or had
Known as home while we were
We felt
So far from

Wherever *might* be
Home and we
Parked the truck or
Car (I forget which) and
Marched right into the
Bright clean sunlit interior
Stainless stainless and
That
Round mirror at the short leg end of the
L-shaped counter so
Characteristic of Valentines the world
(Well mid and southwest)
Over and sat ourselves down on the
Long leg facing the
Stainless steel shelves and
Cobalt blue glass detailing and
Over there in the
Catbird seat you
Might say sat a gent with
Plaid flannel shirt and
Gray beard and some
Kind of slouch hat
(As I recall) and of
Course Levi's who
Looked like he'd
Made himself
Right at
Home

Burritos or
Tortillas I forget which now
Homemade tortillas we
Watched the blonde and blue eyed
Young lady chef make them and
Fell into conversation with the
Grizzled old guy who it
Turns out was from
Originally from
Virginia where he now had a
Studio out in the
Woods on a couple
Acres of land where he

Carved replicas of
Wild
Animals
Quite beautifully too
Judging from the copy of a
Virginia full color glossy paper
Nature or conservation magazine that
Featured an article on him and
That he had there
Copy just casually
Sitting around so he could
Show you
Who
He
Was

And if that wasn't enough he'd
Put a small but
Exquisite carving of a
Bird's wing on the
Counter next to
You
I made
That
That is who
I
Am

So definite
So comprehensible
(To me)
So understandable
With other talents in
Another life I could
Imagine myself
Carving wooden
Totems to the
Creatures we had
Sacrificed to
Fill the world with the
Kind of towns and
Streets where this diner and

I

Usually

Belong.

Skin

No one seemed to be
Interested in speaking
English to us in
Esquibel's Cash Store in
Downtown Tierra
Amarilla, New Mexico also
Known as T/A
They probably *could* speak
English but why
Bother if you don't
Have
To?

So we stood around
Attempting to buy something
Cold to drink and
Walking up and down the
Old wooden aisles among the old
Wooden shelves
Big old fashioned general
Store of the kind you used to
See in every small corner
Crossroads or hamlet
Out in the country but the
Kind of which has become
Just about disappeared as
Better roads bring
Customers to the strip malls and
Enclosed malls and
Super malls with
Lower prices and
Much better selection in
Every city now only some
Few hours drive away in
Most weather in most
Directions from
Just about anybody
Anywhere on a
Paved road in the
Good old

US of A

So we didn't really mind it
That no one was speaking to us in
English in Esquibel's Cash Store in
Downtown T/A that fine morning with the
Sun shining brightly on the
White and yellow vaguely
Spanish colonial style courthouse
Just down the street the only
Other major business if
You could call it that in
Downtown T/A where you could
See the remains in fallen down slowly
Rotted or burned or blown down to the
Ground old wooden buildings
Just up the street or down
Unlike Esquibel's Cash Store
Bright white in its new coats of
Paint and unlike the
Courthouse
County courthouse
Freshly painted in that warm cream and
White and polished spic and
Span inside
The floors
The windows
A
Credit to the community as was
Reies Lopez Tijerina
Brown Power leader for the
Late 1960s charged with
Shooting up or bringing down or
Otherwise creating mayhem in that
Northern New Mexico county
Part of one of the
Old Mexican land grants that had
Been largely ignored and then dished out to
Wealthy (or made wealthy by
The dish out) *anglo* americans after the
Mexican American war in the
1840s

Halls of Montezuma and all
That and you better believe that the
Hispanic people who'd been living
There for several centuries before
That land grab well they
Never
Ever
Forgot
It

So Tijerina in that
Late 1960s period of
Civil unrest and assertion of
Previously ignored civil
Rights by misused and abused
Minorities *not* excluding the
Hispanic people of
Northern New Mexico where all the
Grazing land that they had
Previously held in common for the
Community benefit was
Enclosed in the great capitalist
Tradition beginning in Great Britain in the
Early 18th century
Wiping out all those poor cottagers
No place to graze their
Sheep anymore and then
Damned if the descendents of
Those same Englishmen
Didn't do the same damn thing to the
Entire continent of
North America
They just said
All this land
(Continent really)
That you benighted and
Unsophisticated and non-
Protestant peoples have
Mistakenly imagined to
Belong to all of you
In common
For the

Common good
All these happy grazing and hunting and
Farmlands that you in your
Ignorance of capitalist
Avarice have assumed
Belong to all of you
Forever
For as long as the
Sun shall shine and the
Grass shall grow
Well
Guess what
We have news for you
We can't find your
Title to it in any of
Our records and also in the
Name of the (Protestant)
God we're taking it
All
Away
From you
Course let us note that the
Franciscans had
Done pretty much the
Same damn thing but with
Far less efficiency
Several centuries
Earlier in
Selected parts of the
Southwest and the
Indios who
Resisted the opportunity to
Work for the missions for
Free were allowed to
Starve
Elsewhere

So along about 1967 the
Hispanic people of
Northern New Mexico
Got fed up and started
Something of an insurrection and

Tijerina got
Popular and they were
Going to try his people in
That court but the
Proceedings were
Interrupted by 20 armed men
Including Tijerina who
Shot up the courthouse and
Wounded a couple
Sheriff's deputies and
Eventually Tijerina was
Indeed
Tried and
Found innocent and
Looking now at the
Courthouse walls in
Downtown T/A
Freshly painted
Inside and out
We couldn't even
See where the
Bullet holes had
Been

No matter we
Noticed a middleaged
Man loading fencing
Materials into the
Back of his station
Wagon outside
Esquibel's Cash Store and
Asked him
Being nosy tourists
Who he was and
What was he doing there
Eduardo P. Atencio
One of those so-called
Hyphenated americans and
After all who is pure and
Who isn't and
What is an
Accent

Grew up in T/A
Been a shepherd
Served in the
Navy during the
Korean War and now
Taught English in Espanola and the
University in
Albuquerque you can't
Make a living in these
Small towns anymore
Unless you work for the
County or the
State

Atencio an old
Spanish name from
Altamira where the
Caverns are and
Just what is skin color
Anyway and he pulled his
Watchband away from his
Wrist to show me
Just how light
Where the sun
Didn't strike
His skin remained and he
Held it
Next to mine
You see
He said

But I couldn't
Help thinking that
All things considered
If I had my choice
And in that
Climate
I'd prefer

Brown

Skin.

Red

Chama, New Mexico
Not much of a town
Not even the usual
Rocky Mountain
Boomtown gone
Derelict
A couple fires a couple
Decades apart took
Care of that
Picturesque
Possibility

Not much to do at
Night
They sorta roll the
Sidewalks up
Except for
Foster's
Foster's bar
Down the east end of
Town
Built and quite possibly in
Continuous operation since
1881
The old railroaders' bar
Rooms upstairs from the
Bar arranged for
Well
In the tax rolls they
Called them
Boarding houses
I wouldn't be at all
Surprised if Foster's at
Various times for
Varying lengths of
Time
Quite possibly
Much of the time
Offered services
Certain services

What did you expect from a
Bar directly across the
Street from the
Railroad

Red light districts
Got their name from the
Red lanterns railroad
Brakemen would hang
Outside the resorts they
Frequented so the
Crew callers would know
Where to find them when they were
Wanted down at the
Railroad
Yard

Wouldn't be surprised about that
About Foster's in fact would be
Surprised if anything else were
True but we aren't
Thinking about that when we
Sidle up to
Foster's bar one late
November or early
December
Evening
Maybe 6 PM
Maybe 7
What else you
Gonna do when you're
Staying in a
Dull motel not the
Hunters' cabins down by the
River and the
Rest of the town
Rolls up the
Sidewalks

You're up there
Way up there
Way way up there in the

Mountains of northern
New Mexico where
Anything can happen
Anything
And does
Something of a
Law unto themselves
Up there
Nice people
Mostly
Don't get me wrong but
It's their town and
Visitors are
Tolerated for the income and
Occasional diversion but the
Place definitely hasn't
Turned itself into an
Amusement
Park

Sidled up to the bar and a
Skinny guy in a plaid shirt
Sidles down
Welcome to take his
Place
Make room for two
George Nuño
Bartender
Makes us welcome
Tilted table he jokes with the
Jicarilla senorita in
Plaid shirt and
Big brass belt buckle
Don't fool with this dame
Who has been knocking
Billiard balls into
Pockets and now starts
Knocking them
Down

So far so good and I'm

Sitting there writing down the
Local witticisms for
Posterity
Sometimes that little spiral
Notebook inspires more
Wit and sometimes it
Quiets them
Down

The two Jicarilla ladies and
George
From whom I think they
Take their cue
Don't seem to mind
Helps that we've already
Met George's sister
Rebecca
Last time around and she
As I now tell George
Told us about the
Ghosts upstairs the
Lady suicide the
Cowboy and the
Old Jicarilla who
Used to listen to them
Crying laughing
Silent with terror at their
Fate while he sat at that
Little table
Downstairs
The small one
Round

Plaid shirt's
Putting
Too many down and
George asks for her
Keys
Her car keys before he'll
Pour her another
Round

Ghosts
My mother thought they were
All ghosts
She saw them
Heard them
George tells us

Plaid agrees
Yeah
What a
Sound

Some *anglo* couple wanders in
Guy
Believe it or not makes a
Wetback joke and his
Wife hustles
Hustles him out of that
Bar before he's
Run out of the
Town

Rest of us just
Pretend we didn't
Hear *nada*
None of us
Wants that kind of
Sound

Then while I'm
While we're
Just minding our own business
Talking ghosts with
Plaid who wants her
Keys back but
George holds his
Ground
While we're listening for that
Silence in the
Quiet bar this mid-30s I'd guess
Handsome

Handsome
Hombre sidles in and
For some reason
Not at first
Obvious to me he
Plants himself right
Down beside my
Wife despite there being
Several other empty bar stools
Not next to an accompanied woman that
He could have
Found

Happened so fast and so
Unexpectedly that I
Hadn't time to be
Surprised when he asks her
You're with him?

Meaning
Yo

And then
How come?
With a frown

I ask
Who're you?

No, my turn
Now

Then to her

Why are you married?

Love
She replies

And
How long?

And on and on and
On

Pays for his booze
The good stuff
With a $100 bill
Placed
On the bar
Face
Down

Bartender George with
Great care tells him
Give me a minute
Change upstairs
While Plaid
Put another one
Down

All writers are
Egotists the
Hombre tells me
He paints
Like Picasso
Toulouse Lautrec
Abstract
Too bad they're all
Dead

Just looking for an
Excuse to

Paint my

Town

Red.

Rock

Book Cliffs stood upright to the
North of I-70 west of
Grand Junction, Colorado and into
Eastern Utah
Book Cliffs rising in beiges with a
Band of gold
Tome after matched tome
Upright and formidable
Black band of horizontal
Sedimentary rock for the
Title on the spine
Book Cliffs
Well
They looked like
Book Cliffs
Anyone could see that
Not literature no
Author's completed works but
Law volumes
One massive matched volume
After another in a
Long row standing on the
Bookshelf of the
Mostly flat and very dry
Colorado River valley or
Maybe an old
Complete set of
Mining engineering from
Say
1910
Beige cloth
Gold bands
Black background on
Each spine at exactly the
Same place
Long black and gold and
Beige bands rather than
Successive layers of
Arid sedimentary rock
Cliffs rising perpendicular

Out of the valley
Your standard western
Infinitely deep blue sky
Overhead
Book Cliffs
All that western literature in which I
Could read not a word
Couldn't even remove a
Volume from the
Bookshelf without
Upsetting the massive boulders
Crumbling from rimrock
You saw piles of them
Crashed down at the bases of the
Book Cliffs and
There I was
Searching sky
Searching highway
For some kind of sign while
All that learning
Resided
Unavailable
(To me
Anyway) in that

Dry

Rock.

Neighbors

You're in Nevada
Now
It's not a town
Just the
Border Inn

Lunch counter on the
Utah side
Gambling on the
Nevada

No One Under 21
Near The SLOTS

Two little kids
Maybe 3rd and 4th
Grade at the
Counter

I have to order some
Things to go I
Have to stay
Home I have
Bronchitis

Cheeseburger
Grilled cheese and
French fries

Rhonda asks
How's the road

Older girl:
They have it
Backed up to the
Picnic area
We had to wait
Twenty minutes
Yesterday

JoAnn asks the
Younger girl
Oh, you've got
Bronchitis
Too

Rhonda says
It's not in the
Atlas

I live up the valley
28-29 miles on a
Gravel road

What do they do?

A little ranching
A little cattle grazing
Some people say it's
Desolate
It grows on
You
The
Stars

And we
Sat outside at a
Picnic bench on the
Utah side or
Maybe it was
Nevada

Ate our sandwiches to the
Sound of the
Wind in the
Tree
Overhead
Dry leaves
Rustling against
Each
Other

And you heard the
Tumbleweed
Rolling over the
Grains of
Sand

Just the wind
In the tree and
Dry sticks over that
Bare
Ground

All the way
From Utah to
Nevada
It's just the
Border Inn it's
Not a town

And up the
Valley
29 miles
You've got the

Stars

For

Neighbors.

Berlin

You're the only
One here?

Apart from the snakes
I get headaches from
Looking down

How did you get sent to
Berlin, Nevada?

I did a lot *of*
Naughty
Things the
Ranger
Confided

All alone in a
Ghost town where
Time moved out about
1912
They just closed the
Doors
Leaving unmade
Beds behind
Them

And the icthyosaurs
Don't forget the
Icthyosaurs
Swimming dinosaurs 60 feet long
Left vertebrae so big that the
Miners used them
(The disks) for
Dining

Pour those beans onto a
Disk
Scrape it clean and
Throw the disk
Behind

You

Now Thomas opens the
Park
Conducts the
Tours when
Visitors
Show up
Trailing clouds of
Where are we?

The guidebook says
Tours every
Two hours
Beginning 10 AM I
See people racing
Across that
Desert busting
Axles
Blowing
Tires

I tell them the
Dinosaurs aren't
Going anywhere
They've been
Here for
200 million
Years

Thomas explains
Tucking in his shirt
Mentions *paperwork* but I
Suspect we disturbed his
Siesta

So we look at the
Old mill old cabins old
General store and
Company offices
Then drive up the
Hill to the

Icthyosaurs where
Thomas sweeps out a
Dead flicker

Gone the way of the
Icthyosaurs where
We shall
Eventually
Join them

Cause we've *all* done
Lots of naughty
Things—
Busted axles
Blown tires—
On our

Way to

Berlin

Nevada.

Bodie

Good, by God
We're going to
Bodie or

Goodbye, God
We're going to
Bodie

No one really knew what that
Perhaps
Probably
Apocryphal minister's little
Daughter
Actually
Said

But here we were
Juddering over the
Washboard road
They kept it a
Washboard dirt road
Discourage casual
Vandals on the
Road to
Bodie

End of the road to
Bodie was
More like it
Long road to
Bodie was
More like it

Ghost town
Another ghost town I'd
Fallen for hard
Ghost towns
Places where time had
Stopped

Everyone gone
Elsewhere because that was
How I'd felt
Some of the time
Much of the time

Lost myself somewhere
Back there on the
Road to
Bodie

Lost myself same way
Most everyone
Well
Many people
Lose themselves on the
Road to
Bodie

Pursuing some kind of
Dream of some kind of
Wealth
Greed
Really
Had it all
All I needed
Anyway
Had *her* on the
Seat beside
Me

Didn't see that
Thought we needed
More
More money
Bigger house
Fancier cars
Security
Such as it isn't
That mirage on the
Road to
Bodie

Thought I'd write
Something
Not a poem
No gold rush for
Poetry
Not now
Not ever on the
Road to
Bodie

Rushed all those
Places and
Found nothing
Saw nothing on that
Black highway that was the
Road to
Bodie

Sought the signs saw
Nothing
Learned *nothing*
Nothing but that I'd
Learn nothing
(Which may be
Perhaps worth
Knowing) on the
Road to
Bodie

Drawn to where there was
No one or
Almost no one on the
Road to
Bodie

Looking for
Someone
Myself of course the
Usual
Get rich quick on the
Road to

Bodie

Washboard road all those
Corrugations you go
Up and down as much as
Forward on the
Road to
Bodie

Round the bend
Over the hill
Then you see the
Town what
Remains of the
Town at the
End of the
Road to
Bodie

Nine thousand people lived there
Mostly men they're
Usually the
Bigger fools
Freezing in winter
Frying in summer on that
Desolate ridge
No trees
No water
Water piped in
Wooden box pipes from
Miles away to that
Town at the end of the
Road to
Bodie

The *Bad Man From*
Bodie was in fact
Many men
No shortage of
Losers wanting to
Win at the end of that

Road to

Bodie

Good, by God
We're going to
Bodie

Goodbye, God
We're going to
Bodie.

Underground

Sign
Big sign
Way above the road
Way above the lake
Walker Lake with its
Receded shoreline
Very receded
Shoreline
So receded it took you a
Moment to connect the
Sign there its
Ship's wheel and mention of a
Marina and cocktails restaurant and
Bar and the
Lake which lay shining
Dimly in the starlight
No moon that
Night
And the package store
Closed just about two
Minutes after we
Pulled into the
Campground I
Guess you could
Call it that
Dirt parking lot with
Picnic benches and a
Clean
Spotlessly clean
Facility which was what
Persuaded us to
Spend the night
There
Eight miles from
Hawthorne, Nevada site of a
Huge Navy or perhaps Air Force or
Perhaps all of them
Government ammunition

Dump
Stockpile
Bunkers like giant
Burial mounds dotting the
Landscape
Hundreds of them
Full of munitions and a
Factory in the middle of it all
Right in the middle of
Town making more munitions
Middle of nowhere
Good place to
Blow up if you're
Going to blow up
No one else around
Except the town and the
Town was just glad for the
Jobs there
Hawthorne an old
Railroad town that the
Railroad left early
Track relocation in 1905
Grateful for the various bombs artillery shells and
God knows what else they
Manufactured there since
I think the
Depression
Manna from the
Pork barrel and
Certainly far more
Attractive than these
Little white well
Not flies
Some kind of moths
Maybe
They don't bite but they
Sure love the
Light
Overhead light in the
Back of the pickup truck as we
Try to make our bed
Bed gets harder

That is
Less comfortable
Every year with the
Same mattress
Can it be that
We've changed?

Bones just don't want to
Lie flat on that
Now that I notice
Thin mattress anymore and
Crawling out of the tailgate in the
Middle of the night just
Doesn't have the
Charm it once did if it
Ever did which I
Doubt but
Somehow it
Seems as if
These days at
Night we have to
Get up more
Not the indignity I
Mind so much as the
Clambering over the
Tailgate and
Climbing down the bumper just to
Relieve myself in the
Middle of the night
Clean facility though
Lady who owns the
Campground says she's from
NoDak or was it
SoDak so she feels
Right at home with us
Minnesotans and I'm
Not going to
Put her wiser that we're
Not really
Not in our own minds
Yet
Maybe never

Minnesotans or even
Midwesterners cause
She feels better
Much better
Knowing she's got some
Basic trustworthy clean
No surprises no weirdness
Midwesterners in her
Campground sleeping in the
Back of their nearly new and
Undented pickup truck
Not vagrants
Not drifters
Just nice middle class types who
Like to carry their
Bedroom with
Them

Carried the bedroom with them
But not the liquor cabinet and
You know
After all those
Miles and all the
Excitement of all the
New places and people of
Berlin, Nevada
Population 1 for
Instance
We need
I need
Some booze and if
We drive to
Hawthorne, Nevada now with the
Bed in the back
All made up
It'll get dusty
So we're sitting there in the
Dark with the light out
(Discourage those moths) when I
Think about asking the
People next door in that
Big silver Avion if

By any chance they've
Got some spare
Booze

Knock on their door
(Well, side of the trailer
Don't want to
Knock on their
Screen door)
Guy about our age
Answers

Introduce ourselves
A couple bottles of
Beer we could buy to
Sedate ourselves

Maybe it's
Not the mattress
Nor the excitement of
Berlin, Nevada
Population 1
Maybe it's the
Little white bugs or the
Dry receded lakebed that has
Turned into gravel and dust or
Maybe it's the combination of all
Three or four that has
Somehow put us into this
Mood this
Needy mood and the
Man in the trailer
Sportshirt
Khakis
Elderly parents inside
Suburban attached to the
Trailer outside says
No beer but
I've got a
Bottle of vodka and
7-Up if you'll
Be my guests

Name's Dwight Mace

Invites me to
Set em up on the
Picnic table his
Dad had a stroke so he's
Driving the parents to their
Summer home a
Camp somewhere around
Lake Tahoe they
Spend winters in
Arizona and
Dwight himself
Divorced
Teenage and
Near teenage boy and
Girl
Dwight's a dealer at one of the
Reno casinos
No wonder
I think
He doesn't mind
Strangers but
Westerners can be like that
Anyway
Big country
Small population
You aren't overrun by
Other people
Especially not as I
Think now in a
Walker Lake, Nevada campground with
Little white bugs and
No water
Los Angeles takes all the
Water they bought up all the
Water rights years ago
You plant a tree they'll
Cut it down
Dwight explains
Which was how the
Would-have-been ritzy

Marina became a
Desert
Camp
Just a few short
Miles from all that

Hard rain

Underground.

Here

Geiger Grade
Again
Sunset
Sun Mountain
(Or Mt. Davidson as it's
More commonly known)
Sky clear that
Beautiful light blue
Evening light you
Get over the
Desert
Nevada desert
Western Nevada within
Sight of the
Sierra Nevada
Some twenty miles away
Across the Carson River
Valley
Twisting and winding
Ten miles per hour up the
Geiger Grade
Locals in a big yank
Behind us anxious to
Get home after a long day
Long summer day
Building trophy homes and
Golf course condos for the
Affluent down in the
Valley
Minden once a sleepy
Farming town with a
Big grain mill now all
Shopping malls and
Three and four car
Garages
Where do they all
Come from they didn't
Make that money
Poisoning coyotes
No they made it all in

California
This here's the
Backwash from
California
You can get three or four
Times the house in Nevada than
Silicon Valley so you
Move out here and
Retire
Play golf on
Irrigated golf courses
Life is good
You've got yours
Jack
But these folks
Passing me on the
Geiger Grade
They don't have that
I can tell that
You can tell by their
Cars
Beaters with no A/C
No *functioning* A/C
A/C quit with the last
Owner or the owner
Before that
Tough driving around in
One hundred degree heat
During the day with
No A/C
Driving their beaters up the
Geiger Grade
Windows open
Deep tans on these guys'
And some girls'
Arms from the
Outdoor work from the
Driving around with the
Windows open that
Steady hot blast of
Desert air at
65 MPH and the

Right front still
Pulling from that
Never entirely fixed night
Collision with that
Mule deer or
Whatever
Bald tires and no
Spare
But there's
Work
Work down in the
Valley building all those
New homes and strip
Malls for the people who live in those
New homes your choice of
McDonald's or Burger King or Taco Bell or
Don't get me going
That once-beautiful valley
Don't get me going and
Where are all these people
Going I ask myself only
Virginia City semi-ghost town of some
800 souls at the end of this road the
Geiger Grade
You don't
Go up the Geiger Grade unless you're
Going to Virginia City because once you
Get there the only thing to do is
Go down
So?
We wonder and the poor people
Hurrying and anxious to
Get home held up
Behind we who do not know the
Road could be more ready to
Run our still pretty new and
Shiny truck off the road
We're holding them up with
No place to pull over till we
Get to Gold Hill
Pull over
Let 'em go

Wherever cause we're
Headed to that little
R/V Park and Campground
New place
Was a new place when we
Stayed there a few
Years before and
Nearly got blown off the
Mountain by that
Washoe Zephyr
So called
Place mostly empty and with a
Good view of the
Graveyard
Had the place
The RV Park to ourselves
That night no need for
Privacy in the back of the
Pickup truck or was it then
Station wagon no
Need for curtains cause there was
No one except maybe
Coyotes and the
Ghost of Julia Bulette
Around

Gold Hill
Over the Divide
Fourth Ward School
D Street
Town seems busier than
Last time but that's
Not surprising it's
Summer now and
Down F and
Turn the corner and
Oh my God
The RV Park and Campground is
Full
No Vacancy that I
Can see and the
Folks in their big old

Motor homes and large old
Battered aluminum
Travel trailers these
Folks look like they're
Settled in for the
Duration
Whatever that might be
Every single camping spot
Filled and then some and
Since the place was
Never more than a
Glorified parking lot
Parking spot
Picnic bench
Parking spot
Picnic bench and
So on these people
With their big old RVs and
Long full time
Trailers have their
Daily drivers
Their cars
Parked everywhere and their
Kids are riding bicycles and
Chasing each other and playing ball and
Whatever else kids do these
Days all over the
Campground
This is where the
Poor people live while they're
Building the big homes and
Working the counters and
Cleaning the floors
Down in the
Valley

The poor people and the
Retired *Full-Time RVers* as they're
Known who sold it all or
Almost all and live out of their
Elaborate or not so fancy
Winnebagos trundling across the

Southwestern United States from one
Campground to the next and
Getting by on small
Pensions and
Social
Security
If it is
Indeed
Security
Nomads
No fixed address
No responsibilities
No community
Post office box
Somewhere well
Some people
Like it
I guess
Not my idea of
Heaven living in a box off the
Ground on four rubber
Tires
Crowded
Campgrounds but then
So what if
They're happy
Well we're
Here now
Our famous refrain for the end of the
Day when you're too tired to
Drive further and you're
Just gonna camp where you've
Landed after all that
Driving
All those miles
And who are we to
Disdain the RVs
Heck
We're sleeping in the
Back of a
Pickup

Truck
So we register at the office
Once a clean but
Spartanly furnished place now
Jam packed with convenience
Goods snacks groceries videos even
Liquor all the comforts of the
Local strip mall for the
Floating but anchored by their
Utility cords and temporary
Plumbing population and
When you think about it
Far better Virginia City with its
Spectacular views and
Wide open spaces all
Around than some
Godforsaken trailer
Park somewhere by a
Highway
Kids seem happy
Anyway
One little girl
Nearly rides her
Bicycle into the
Front end of our
Vehicle
Neighbor next door
That is to say
Just a picnic bench away
But he's removed the
Picnic bench to
Give himself room to
Park his ancient Dodge
Power wagon beside his
Trailer
We know what they're
Eating for supper and
Watching on
Television
Introduce ourselves
Nice people he
Moves his vehicle

Parks it at the
Campground entrance to
Give us some
Room
Nice people

We're the

Floating population he

Lives

Here.

Embarrassing

Tailgate party sitting
There facing the other
Line of campers
Parked cars and RVs and
Trailers across the
Circle of asphalt in that

Geiger Grade
Again
Maybe one more
Time we slept going
Back there
Back to
Virginia City drawn by
By the
Place
Must have been the
Place
Didn't really
Know anybody there
Except Jack Curran
Reba Tawks
Both in their 70s
Both musicians
Reba making do with her
Widow's mite as she
Called it and
Jack with his pot of
Silver dollars that
Someone stole from
Underneath his floor one day an
Inside job if there
Ever was one
But happy
Happy in their own way
Part of that little town
Clinging to the edge of
Sun Mountain and
Populated as much by
Ghosts all those

Dead and gone
Miners   '
Dead and gone
Whores and fancy men and
Ordinary Joes and Josephines
But
But really you can't say
You're among Joes and Josephines if you
Even bother to live in
Virginia City because the
Place is
Different
Different at the height of its
Silver mining glory and
Different now because of its
Silver mining glory and
Different
Different if only because it
Clings there to that
Mountain every street a
Story higher or lower than the
Next and the entire
Place a twenty mile winding
Mountain road from the
Valley where everything
Everything was easier except
Seeing the stars at
Night or feeling as if you
Belonged to a small town a
Community of
People who
Knew and
Cared for
Each other
Some of them
Many of them
Bad apples and losers and
Loners everywhere
We built a cabin for the
Town veteran
Shell-shocked since
Vietnam

Lives on charity and
Rarely washes
Lives out on that
Ridge somehow his
Old cabin
Burned down
Jack told me
Reba there at the
Top of A Street
See forever but a
Hard climb up those
Stairs with
Groceries
Playing clubs in
Reno
Carson
Till 2 at night
Driving home
Not easy when you're
Over 70
Still a place
Out there on the
Edge but not
Beyond of
Civilization and we're
There sitting on the
Tailgate of our pickup truck
Eating melons from Green River,
Utah and Italian cold cuts subs with
Fresh baked bread and
Homemade peppers and
Real cotto salami from
Luigi's Deli in
Eureka, Nevada
Population 600 and
There's just one
Camping spot left
Parking place
Really
When a young
Relatively young
Maybe mid-30s

Woman dressed all in
White
White leather jacket with
Fringes and white riding
Chaps and fringes and
Riding a white
Harley Davidson
Hog
As they're known
Rolls into the
Campground with that
Inimitable and would have been
Patented if they could
Patent it sound and
Parks the machine
Right opposite us in that
Last parking spot in the
Campground
Removes jacket
Skin tight white T-shirt
Well filled and
White Levi's and
Rolls out her air
Mattress and props it up
And in the
Heat at the
End of the
Day (it's about
Sunset)
She drops herself
Down
Resting there
Arms beneath her
Watching the world as it has
Gathered itself
Go by in the campground
All alone
Other bikers around
Big Harley rally somewhere
Down in the valley and
Some of them
They're not gonna motel it

They're tough
Outlaws live by
Their own rules and
They're gonna
Tough it out like this
Lady in white on
This mattress
Sleep next to their bikes in
Little tents in
Dirt and asphalt
Campgrounds

Later that evening
We're out
Walking our
Evening stroll down
D Street with all the
Saloons open and
People spilling in and out
Music
Lights in the
Soft Nevada
Dark and there
In the street
Dancing with some
Handsome T shirt and Levi's
Hunk
Dancing arm in arm and
Cheek to cheek we
See the
Lady

Still later we're
Lying in bed in the
Back of the pickup
Truck and overhear
Voices and
Peek outside and
There's a half dozen
Tipsy adults
Wandering past the
Truck and down the

Hill and across the
Gully to the old
Graveyard

Then
Still later but
Not much later the
Sheriff's Cherokee with
Flashing lights
Down there escorting the
Revelers *back from* the
Graveyard
Grateful citizens
Slightly inebriated but
Cooperative thanking the
Sheriff or his deputy and the
Cherokee for depositing them
Back in the
Campground

Lights out

Then AM and
My wife's washing up in the
Campground washhouse
Women's side and
She's chatting with the
Lady in white who
Admires her tattoo and
Long hair and
Edie asks her *Were*
You with those
Folks evicted from the
Graveyard
Late last night?

And the
Lady in white
Confesses

That was so

Embarrassing.

Up

No sign
No sign on the
Barber shop at all
Not even a barber pole
Not even a barber
First time we
Looked in
Little barber shop
Some kind of
Ripped and faded
Poster displayed
Near the rear of the
Place on some kind of
Stand
Showed different
But not too
Different
Kinds of haircuts on
Various men and
Boys
Kinda thing you'd
Imagine the US Military
Might display for
Guidance to its
Personnel but I
Guessed
But did not know
That this poster was
Intended for guidance
To ensure appropriate
Grooming for the
Male members of all ages of the
Church of Jesus Christ of
Latter-day Saints
Mormons
In other words who
Made up
To judge from the
Size of the *chapel* and the
General air of order and

Rectitude and
Civic pride
Who
As I started to say
Appeared to comprise the larger
Largest
Part of the population of this
Town in the midst of
Irrigated agriculture in an
Otherwise bone dry
Desert in Eastern Utah
Town by the name of
Blanding, Utah
Look it up on the
Map
Pretty much in the
Middle of
Nowhere
Not at the end of the world
But
As the saying goes
You can see it from
There
Which was just the way the
Mormons liked it
They'd gone west to
Get away
Found a city
Entire civilization
Theocratic
Evangelical of
God in the
Wilderness and
That
Without a doubt
They did
Book of Mormon in our
Nightstand drawer back at the
Neat as a pin motel
And on the lawn
Antique agricultural implements and
Machinery

Old tractors old combines old plows
All those early models of
John Deere and Minneapolis Moline and
Fordson and International Harvester and
Quite a few more you never heard of or
Even dreamed of unless
Sometime in the first
Half of the 20th century you
Worked on or near a
Farm

Blanding
Well on the outside
The exterior
The initial superficial
Appearance the place was
Bland
All that civic probity
Streets neatly swept of the
Ever-erasing desert dust
Right there
Right beyond the
Edge of town the
Desert began and
Don't you ever
Forget it the
Only *white* people who ever
Really pulled off agriculture
Only people who could possibly have
Pulled off agriculture in the
Middle of that desert were the
Mormons because
Desert agriculture
Required irrigation which
Demands strict and hierarchical and
Centralized control
Which
Through the
Church of Jesus Christ of Latter-day Saints
They had
And which the Navajo
Herdsmen

Semi nomadic
Never liked towns
Did not

It's evening and we're
Walking along those
Neatly swept sidewalks
Sidewalks!
Enjoying the feeling of
Smooth pavement under our
Soles
Souls?
And here we are
Middle aged husband and wife
Walking along and probably the
Cultural cues that would
Tell just about any
Mormon that we don't belong
Are not
Strictly speaking
One with them
Are not members of the Church of Jesus Christ of
Latter-day Saints
Stuff that
In other words
Would be obvious to the
(White) locals
Our longish
Hair
(Longer than anything offered as a
Choice in that poster in the
Barbershop)
Her no bra
My no socks and penny loafers
Anybody white from there
Would immediately know we're not
From there

But that doesn't matter to a Native American
I assume Navajo
Kid or couple kids in a
Beatup little Toyota who

Turn around in a parking lot
Adjacent to the
Sidewalk where we're walking
(By now it's dark) and who
For no immediately obvious
Personal reason that
She or I can
Think of
Leans out of the
Car window and
Says to us
I assume he meant us
Looking at us
No one else around
He says

Look at yourselves

If you think we're

Fucked

Up.

Lost Cause

Roundhouse Books
Right there on the Main Street of
Downtown Delta, Colorado
Out there on the Western Slope
(Of Colorado) in the middle of the
Middle of nowhere
More or less
Delta an agricultural town which was
Some twenty miles from
Montrose, Colorado which was itself
Not exactly a
Metropolis
But Montrose
As I now recalled had
Two bookstores a county seat and the
Best shopper weekly newspaper
The *San Juan Horseshoe*
Pure satire
In the entire country
But I digress
Roundhouse Books was
Right there on the
Main Street of
Delta, Colorado where we
Walked in the dry I guess it
Must have been autumn or perhaps
April cold
Spitting snow
Occasionally but
Warm enough
Just warm enough in our
Polarfleeces underneath
Levi's jackets
Not that we looked like the
Cowboys and cowgirls
Didn't have the tans or the walk or the
Talk and anyway this was more
Farming than ranching country
Out here
Irrigated farming

Send produce all over the
World
Japan, Thailand, as
Marvin Ryan tells me
Tells us in the
C&J Café
Also right there on the
Main Street of
Downtown Delta, Colorado
Big bustling café full of
Locals hunched over hot coffees and
Hot meals
Lots of homemade food in
That café and now that I
Think of it this was a
Saturday and you had a lot of the
Locals coming in
Weekly shopping in town
Done and now they're
Relaxing and catching up with
Each other at the
End of the week
Did not strike me as a
Mormon town
Not exclusively or mainly
You saw all those old VWs there out on the
Edge of town by some
Colorfully or you might say
Picturesquely painted or
Unpainted housing
Several VWs
Both mobile and otherwise
Complete and semi-
Dismembered for their
Parts in front of each house
And at that time
That part of that decade
In that part of the world
That is
Anywhere out west
Rural west where they
Didn't salt the roads and

You didn't need an effective heater or
Defroster
(Those old VWs had neither)
You'd see old VWs still being
Run by people who had bought them
Years or decades earlier when they
Were *Goin up Country*
As Canned Heat so
Memorably put it and
Bought cheap land that at the
Time nobody wanted and they
Made a life for themselves
Using a minimum of cash and a
Maximum of ingenuity
Hippies
You might say but in
Truth you can't make it
Out there in the sticks unless
You're pretty industrious
You gotta be able to
Figure out how to make a
(Hopefully) legal or semi
Legal living (pay and accept
Cash) and be your own
Mechanic which in the
Case of VWs did not
Take much you just
Acquired John Muir's
How to Keep Your
Volkwagen Alive A
Manual of Step-by-Step
Procedures for the
Compleat Idiot and
Following John
You rebuilt those little
Flat opposed 4
Air cooled motors just about
Anywhere it was
Convenient
For instance your
Kitchen table or your
Kitchen floor

That took care of
Transportation and you
Grew or shot a lot of your
Own food and
Well
You get the picture and
You know what
From the perspective of
Twenty years on the day shift
The golden chains of a pension
You might or might not get
While they worked you harder and
Paid you a bit less in
Constant dollars every year
From that perspective
Maybe
Alternative wasn't such a
Bad way to
Go
Too late for us
Of course
We sorta started out that way
Built the house
Our own house
Tiny place 400 square feet
But then she got a real job
What was *supposed* to be
Temporary turned into a
Real job and my
Removal to temp work
Which was *supposed* to be
Temporary turned into a sorta chronic
Long term thing
And now here we are
Drivin around in a
New Dodge pickup
Because we can afford it
(So long as it lasts 20 years) and
Well
Then again
We're 50 and
Still sleeping in the

Back of a pickup so
Maybe
We're not yet a

Lost

Cause.

Come

Saguaro cactus
Green painted
Rather rectilinear
Seeing as it was
Made up from
Sections of
Prefabricated
Round fence posts
The kind with the
Holes drilled in them at
Regular intervals to
Accept the rails
Well
With this cactus
The holes held the
Arms for the
Saguaro
Not a large saguaro
A small saguaro a
Junior saguaro
I suppose
Maybe four feet high
(Those fence posts only
Grow so tall) and
Marking the otherwise
Unmarked dirt road
Where we'd been instructed to
Turn to reach
After a suitable
Stretch of unpaved
High desert rangeland
Dirt road just east of the
Front Range
Just east of Pike's Peak
(Which rose majestically in the
Distance) and
Not far from the
Phantom Canyon Road
Leading west
Up into the mountains to that

Ancient gold mine ghost town
Not yet turned into a
Casino heaven known as
Cripple Creek
Out there in the high arid
Rangeland
Semi desert
See for miles
Pike's Peak
Maybe 30 miles away and
See forever east toward
Kansas in the other
Direction and see forever
South toward Raton Pass and
New Mexico in *that*
Direction
North and you were headed toward
Denver
But right there
Right where we were
Somewhere near Penrose
Near Florence, Colorado among the
Sagebrush and prickly pear and
Bunchgrass and where they had
Once found oil and then
Kept drilling and
Found water
Hot water and
Lots of it
So much so that it was
Not useful to Conoco but
Someone bought the place for
That hot mineral water and
Isolation
Twenty acres of
Nothing all around you to the
Next ranch and
Out there
What with the
Hot water and the
Privacy and the
Sunlight almost year round

They built a pool to hold the water
Two pools
Actually
One shallow so you could
Sit in it
Quite large and
Another deep but
Very hot
Where the water first
Emerged and they
Put up some
Fairly shacky little
Changing rooms and
Offered their resort to the
Public under the
Sobriquet of
Typical western name with that
Combination of self-mockery and
Humor at the expense of the
Pretentious
Called themselves
As I started to say the
Desert Reef Beach Club

And
Well
You know
Mention the ocean
That part about the *reef*
That part about the *beach*
And we're *there*
Drawn to the
Thought and smell and
Touch of salt water which
The *beach*
The *reef*
You might reasonably expect
Out there in the high desert
Rangeland of eastern
Colorado within sight of
Pike's Peak and the

Front Range
I guess we just sort of assumed that
Some kind of high tide
Well
Honestly
No
We knew it was
Artesian hot water and
We knew also that the
Sartorial expectations at that
Place were a little bit
Different than most other
Places in that their
Policy
Their practice was
What you or
If not you
Then they called
Clothing optional
Meaning
Go nude if you
Want to which
When you think of it
Was what most people I
Would
You would expect
Want to do
Given that there are a
Rather finite number of
Establishments
Even in a place like
Colorado where
You can do that
Sort of
Thing

Tell you this much
We'd never been to
That kind of *place* before and
We're not entirely sure how we
Thought about it
Been skinnydipping with

Friends of course
Backyard pools at night and the
Occasional skinnydipping with
Friends in some private cove in a
Lake or stream or shore but a
Place specifically
Set aside
Where you'd meet
Strangers
Well
No
We hadn't done that
But
You know
We're
Ready to
Because we'd come around to the
Idea that people *weren't* the
Clothes they wore nor were they the
Cars they drove nor were they the
Houses (or lack of housing) they lived in
Nor were they the schools nor the
Universities that they had
Attended or not
Attended nor were they the
Sum of money they had on
Deposit in the bank or
Invested (wisely or not) in the
Stock market or some kind of
Mutual fund or
Real estate investment trust or
Offshore private bank or
Hedge fund
Nor in their
Sock or under their
Cabin floor
And we'd come to the
Conclusion that
People
Some people
Suffer an excess of
Delusion in their own

Material grandeur and
Tax laws designed to
Reward the rich and punish the poor
Made it ever easier for
Some folks to debauch
Themselves in a
Saturnalia of acquisition while
Other folks wondered
Quite a few other folks
Wondered if they'd
Ever be able to buy a house or
Drive a decent car while
Making do on the
Minimum
Wage
We'd come to the
Conclusion
In other words
That you aren't the
Stuff you own and
That in fact the
Poor people
The truly poor people
Were those who had
So much stuff that their
Property owned them and the
Next poorest people were the
Deluded fools who
Yearned to live in that
Same
Condition

But enough
This is an
Old story and
Our contribution was
Only to recognize that the
Gilded Age was once more
Upon us and to
Try to figure out how to
Escape its grasp and so
As we ran and ran

Drove that
Black highway from
One end of the
Continent to another
Always looking for a
Sign
Where to go
Where did we
Belong
Where was
Something that
Might be called
Home
Or
Refuge
Or
Shelter from the
Storm of a
Society gone mad in its
Own greed and
Narcissism
In other words
We had
Been to
Bodie
By God
We'd been
Looking for a sign and the
Middle aged Hispanic guy at the
Small crossroads
Convenience store on the
Outskirts of
I forget
Or never knew
Either Penrose or
Florence
We'd stopped and asked
How to find the
Desert Reef Beach Club and he
Smiled an understanding but
Not judgmental smile
Just that hint of a shared

Secret knowledge and
Told us to
Cross the bridge
Turn left and
Look for the
Green wooden
Saguaro

Which we did
Had done
And now here we were
Driving very slowly over the
Rutted dirt road among the
Hillocks and sagebrush and
Passing the occasional
Very occasional
Ranch house
Following signs when we came to
Places where the
Road forked
Following the forks with the
White hand painted signs
Marked *DRBC*
Until
Up ahead of us on a
Level stretch of ground we
Saw a half dozen parked cars
None of them looking
Particularly new or
Spiffy and behind that a
Board fence and behind that a
Somewhat shacky looking little
Office and the
Sign
The Sign
One of them that
We had been
Looking for
Desert Reef Beach Club
Proof if you ever
Needed proof that
Your destination or at least

What appears to be your
Destination does not always
Look exactly like
What you thought it
Would but we were
Undeterred we had
Not expected luxury
The point was never
Not for us
Luxury and if
For you the
Point is
Luxury well then
You can
Stop reading
Or listening
Right here though I
Suspect that if for you the
Point was luxury you would have
Stopped reading not
Long after you
Began
Somewhere way back
Way way back say in
California
Right near the coast
Which even then was
Not
In a relative way
Luxury
Not the kind of
Luxury you can buy
Because
You know what
A little bit too
Much of that and you
Can't feel anything
Anymore
You go numb to
Yourself and to
Others
You don't feel

The wind
The water
The sun on
Your skin
Nor see it in
Others
You see the
Stuff you've got on and the
Stuff they've got on an
Elaborate language of
Superficiality
The court of the
Sun King all over again
Dumbed down for the
Masses
But I digress
We'd parked
Closed the truck doors
Walked to the office where a
Deeply suntanned and grayhaired
Gent tells us
Why don't you
Walk through there and
Take a look
Make sure it's
What you have in mind
Before I
Take your
Money

We'd never engaged in this
Kind of thing before but
Yes we began to
We had a
Good feeling we
Like the look of this
Guy and the unpretentious
Look of the facility and
Yes we thought it could be
Very easily done
Just put a desert reef out
There in the sun

But I digress
Though we had in fact
Passed Highway 61
The road to Hibbing
The road to the Delta at the
Beginning of our
Journey west
And yes
We walked through the
Portals
And old road
The board fence
The ramshackle office
And there beyond
Twice ten acres of
Not particularly fertile ground with
Neither walls nor towers were
Girdled round and in fact
Neither the men nor women nor
Children we saw before us
Lounging around or
Soaking in the pool were
Girdled round with
Anything
They had
In other words
No clothes on

No clothes on and I'd say
I'd have to say
You might not say but
I'd say they
Looked beautiful
White skin
Brown skin
Very tanned white
Skin
Not a lot of
People this was a
Weekday
Weekday afternoon
But a couple there with

Two small kids and a
Woman deeply tanned all
Languor and grace at the
Far end of the pool and a
Couple guys looked like they'd
Worked outside all their
Lives and have now gotten tans
Where the
Sun hadn't tanned before
Tattoos
Or not
Well muscled and
Trim
Or not
Your cross section of
Unpretentious humanity on a
Sunny but high overcast
Just east of the
Front Range
Colorado
Afternoon

What do you think?
I asked her and

Looks good to
Me
She replied

2.

Bright green leaves
Wound on a thin vine
From her thigh to her
Abdomen and down the
Other thigh
Salmon pink flowers with
Yellow and purple
Centers blossomed along the
Vine amid the green
Leaves and a single
Bright blue moth
Flew between her
Pelvis and her
Belly button
Got people's attention
That tattoo did
But of course at
That place out in the
Eastern Colorado
Desert they were
Polite enough
Not to stare and
Only eventually
After we moved over to the
Hot water pool where
There were more
People and your
Presence there
Indicated an
Inclination to be
Sociable did
People really
Ask about it

Ten years ago now
Wasn't even
Legal in
Massachusetts at the
Time

I did I
Drew the lines with
Ball point pen and the
Tattooist filled them in with
Colors

Never failed to
Amaze or
Please me how
She became so
Much more
Herself
So much more at
Ease when she
Removed her
Clothes until
With nothing on
She seemed
Utterly
Relaxed and
Confident
No longer shy
Joyful
Happy
Confident
Outgoing
Some people are
Not meant to
Fit in
Conform
Find their
Preordained place in the
Scheme of things
Her
Joy in
Life in
Living in the
Every day
Hour minute
And not just the
Big things but the

Minutiae
That blue moth
That flower
That green vine
My great fortune in
Life was that
She shared
Could share
Wanted to share
Did share
That joy with
Me

How had I not seen
How could I have not seen
Why did I not know
That with that
Joy you
Never needed to
Go
By God
To Bodie
Nor
Anyplace like
Bodie

I saw now that
That tattoo was
The sign was
Her sign
And it said

Here I am
I've been just
Waiting for

You

To

Come.

Back There